T0161431

Defy Your Diagnosis

Overcome Any Obstacle with the FIT Life Formula

Lorraine Bossé-Smith

Clovercroft Publishing

Defy Your Diagnosis

Published by Clovercroft Publishing, Franklin, Tennessee

Scripture taken from THE HOLY BIBLE, NEW INTERNATIONAL VERSION®, NIV® Copyright © 1973, 1978, 1984, 2011 by Biblica, Inc.™ Used by permission. All rights reserved worldwide.
Scriptures marked KJV are taken from the KING JAMES VERSION (KJV): KING JAMES VERSION, public domain.
Edited by Christy Callahan

Cover and Interior Design by Suzanne Lawing

Printed in the United States of America

978-1-950892-29-7

Disclaimer
Neither the publisher nor the author is engaged in rendering professional and/or medical advice or services to the individual reader. The ideas, procedures, practices, and suggestions in this book are not intended as a substitute for consulting with your physician. All matters regarding your health require medical supervision.

If readers are taking prescription medicines, they should consult with their physicians and not take themselves off prescribed drugs without the proper supervision of a physician. Always consult your physician or qualified health care professional before undertaking any change in your physical regimen.

Neither the author or the publisher shall be liable or responsible for any loss or damage allegedly arising from any information or suggestion in this book.

While the author has made every effort to provide accurate information at the time of publication, neither the publisher or the author assumes any responsibility for errors or changes that occur after publication.

Dedication

God used my mother's death as an instrument to rescue me
from the depths of hell and improve the quality of my life.
As her life was taken, mine was restored.
I was set free!

As I faced two horrifying diagnoses, God held my hand.
When the physical pain was too great, He carried me.
My hope was in Him,
and I am forever grateful for His healing touch!

As tough and determined as I was to *defy my diagnosis,*
I couldn't have survived it all without the love and support of
my best friend and husband, Steve Smith.
We make a great "we"!

Lorraine Bossé-Smith

Contents

Foreword

Dear Reader:

I am a seventy-five-year-old retired minister. Though retired, I am still in the business of counseling people in distress. One of the most common things bringing people to me is the problem of having an illness that doctors don't know how to treat. These people have gone to a variety of doctors, but none seem to know what is really going on or how to treat what is going on. Lorraine Bossé-Smith's book, *Defy Your Diagnosis*, is tailor-made for these people in that it outlines a way to pray for guidance.

Throughout the years, I have discovered there aren't many books that contain new and fresh information. Most are simply a rehash of what you have read and heard before. Going back decades, I can count on one hand the books I have read that contain new or unforgettable information. Defy Your Diagnosis is so far the one book I have read in the last decade that does that for me. I love the three prayer requests Lorraine recommends for people struggling with illnesses that doctors can't seem to get a handle on. The three requests are: (1) *Lord, lead me to a medical partner who understands my condition;* (2) *Lord, give me the courage to follow the advice given to me by this medical partner;* (3) *Lord, be a partner in the treatment given to me.*

I am so enamored by these three guidelines that I have personally purchased over 20 copies of this book to give to people struggling with difficult-to-diagnosis conditions, and I plan to continue buying copies as the Lord leads me. The stories these people have shared with me in regard to these three requests have proved over and over again the wisdom and power of Lorraine's advice.

Even if you don't have a medical condition, I encourage you to read Lorraine's story, which is one of trials, battles, victories, and defeating the odds. With her FIT Life Formula (Foundation of Faith, Insights into Self-Improvement, and Tackling the Tough Stuff) as its foundation, *Defy Your Diagnosis* offers chapters that address each area to allow you to move toward personal and professional success.

My prayer is for your spirit to be lifted, your heart filled with God's love for you, and for the encouragement found in its pages to encourage you on your journey to wellness (emotionally, mentally, physically, and spiritually).

Dr. Gordon Peterson
Loveland, Colorado

Preface

Back in 1996, my entire life came crumbling down upon me. I lost just about everything and almost didn't live to tell about it. My life was completely out of control, and I knew I had to find a better way. I began a quest that ultimately led me to my FIT Life Formula.

My journey of learning and discovering ways to lessen stress and create a healthier life became my business and is still my passion today—to improve the quality of *your* life.

Whether I am speaking, training, coaching, recruiting, consulting, or authoring books, I help people succeed both professionally and personally. We can no longer separate them. I believe what happens at work comes home, and our personal stress impacts our ability to perform at our best. The notion of work-life balance seems impossible to some, but it IS possible when we clearly define what matters most to us and how we want OUR life to look like.

That's where I come in. My principles of a Fit Life not only help you lead and succeed professionally, but they also encourage and motivate you toward a healthier, more balanced life personally. If we are truly going to achieve great things, we must be mentally, emotionally, physically, and spiritually healthy.

These aren't just "pie in the sky" concepts for me. I have lived them out, beating two incurable diseases. Work with me, and you will quickly discover that I genuinely care about you. Your entire life does matter, and I will help you Defy YOUR Diagnosis!

My Not-So-Fit Life

When I speak, I can see the judgment upon people's faces. I often hear statements like, *You have no idea what it is like to be overweight because you are so fit.* Or, *You just seem too perfect. What do you know?* Well, let me tell you about my so-called "perfect" life.

I was born the fifth of five in Hicksville, Long Island, New York, in 1966. I was what they call an OOPS! in a year that went down in the history books. My parents witnessed my oldest sister get married in March, buried my sister Ellen in August, and gave birth to me in October. Needless to say, my parents were numb and lost.

I remember wanting to do things and go places, but my parents were in a fog. Their life force was sucked out of them and only the shell of a body remained. I ended up being a bright spot—a gift from God, as my mom said, making my parents smile and laugh again ... until my thirteenth birthday, when my dad died of cancer. Yes, my dad died *on* my birthday. Nurses took pity on him, however, and marked the death certificate as October 2. He tried so very hard to live and suffered in doing so. To this day, I honor him by celebrating my birthday in a big way.

I was Daddy's little girl, and his death felt like someone ripped my heart out and stomped on it. I couldn't breathe, and I didn't understand how or why God let this happen. This traumatic event not only put me on a spiritual quest, but it formulated my values: integrity, excellence, and honor.

I learned at a very young age that things didn't come easy. My mom and I had to pull ourselves together and continue to live life, even when we didn't feel like it. I began working at the age of thirteen in order to have clothes. In my twenties, I attended night school while working 50 hours a week and paid my own way through college—squeezing those four years into seven! I obtained my associate's degree in OIT and my bachelor's degree in Business Marketing and Communications.

During my corporate-climbing days, I excelled, achieved, and conquered every challenge. I broke records, received awards, and enjoyed financial compensation. Unfortunately, my personal life was a disaster. Although I had titles and prestige, I had no peace. A powerhouse by day, I was physically abused at night. Low self-esteem got me into my predicament, but poor life and stress management kept me there.

My extremely low self-image hurled me from one abusive relationship to the next, marrying the worst abuser of them all. When my mother died of cancer in 1997, I finally had the courage to get out and went through a horrible divorce. The stress of it all about killed me.

I dropped down to 97 pounds at nearly five feet, ten inches tall. I had pencil-thin arms and only 6 percent body fat, which is very unhealthy for a woman. I barely had enough strength to go on, and if it weren't for my steadfast faith, I don't think I would have tried. I embarked on a journey to learn better ways of managing my stress and began to focus on my *total self* for complete health with these Four Pillars: emotional, mental, physical, and spiritual health. Together they form the basis of my FIT Life Formula—a foundation of faith, insights into self-improvement, and tackling the tough stuff.

I got remarried to a wonderful man but then found myself fighting for my life once again. I not only overcame but conquered *two* incurable diseases, which you will read more about in its own chapter. I know firsthand the importance of balancing the Four Pillars. So even though I may appear to have lived an easy, perfect life, I have had to work hard for *everything*. I know pain and suffering; I know heart-wrenching grief; and I know poverty and failing health. Although I may not have walked in your shoes, I understand the uphill climb that seems to never end. I have traveled through the swamp, and I am here to encourage and inspire you!

The FIT Life Formula

My goal is simple. I want to help YOU defy your diagnosis!

Whether you are facing a health or medical crisis, a broken relationship or divorce, job dissatisfaction or loss, death, personal difficulties, or financial struggles, *Defy Your Diagnosis* is here to encourage you. The principles in it utilize the FIT Life Formula and will help you improve your entire life.

I have authored eight other published books (*Leveraging Your Leadership Style with Study Guide, I Want My Life Back, Leveraging Your Communication Style, Leveraging Your Leadership Style* (and workbook), *Fit Over 50, Finally FIT,* and *A Healthier, Happier You*) and a myriad of booklets (https://www.lorrainebosse-smith.com/shop-resources). I write on assignment for a variety of printed magazines, have shared my heart with thousands of radio listeners across the country, and have been on live television shows.

In addition, I am a Certified Professional Behavior Analyst (CPBA) and Certified Professional Motivators Analyst (CPMA). I am also an advanced certified personal trainer and listed in the 2000 *Who's Who of Entrepreneurs* and the 2005 *Who's Who Among Female Executives.* I am a professional speaker with the National Speaker's Association and consult and coach business executives on how to be FIT to Lead and Succeed. Despite all my trials, I love the Lord God with all my heart, soul, and strength. He has been my strength when I could barely walk, and He has been the wind under my wings when I've needed a lift. Because of Him, I was able to defy each and every diagnosis!

I wish I'd had fewer struggles, but then I wouldn't be able to share what I've learned with you. In our darkest times, when we lean in close to the Father, we listen more and grow exponentially. We are molded and shaped in Jesus's image. When we cry out and say, "ENOUGH! I cannot take any more," we're in good company, for He suffered beyond understanding so that we may have eternal peace.

Thank you for picking up a copy of this book! I'm honored to share my story and principles with you. My hope is that through my story, you will realize you aren't alone. My prayer is that my FIT Life Formula will remind you how precious, special, and unique you are and that you are worth a healthy, happy, fulfilled, and FIT Life!

Each chapter addresses at least one component of the FIT Life Formula: a Foundation in Faith, Insights into Self-Improvement, or Tackling the Tough Stuff. Some chapters may cover more than one area. Feel free to read the chapter that speaks to you first or go front to back. The end-of-chapter questions are designed to bring home the principles shared and allow you to apply them to your own life. There is no right or wrong way to use this resource.

May the lessons I have learned and principles shared here help you defy YOUR diagnosis and get your life back!

Lorraine Bossé-Smith
www.lorrainebosse-smith.com

p.s. If you would like to receive monthly encouragement and support for your FIT Life, sign up for my FREE FIT Life newsletter at my website listed above. Just add your first and last name along with your email address and look for an opt-in email from me to officially register. **I do not sell my lists.** You will receive my monthly newsletter, as well as a special product offer per month and an inspirational message.

Get Back Up When Life Knocks You Down

*You do what you can for as long as you can, and when you finally can't,
you do the next best thing. You back up but you don't give up.*

~ CHUCK YEAGER ~

Pilot

My life can best be described as a journey. I have walked a lot of miles
and crawled my way through some tough times. I believe the saying,
"God doesn't give us more than we can handle." I have often wondered, though, if He got me confused with someone else, because I
doubted whether I would survive my circumstances; the pain was too
great and the burden too heavy. You may have felt the same way at
some point in your life. In fact, I *know* you have.

Life Is Not Easy

Since the beginning of time, life has been tough. Remember, the
American dream only promises us the opportunity for life, liberty,
and the *pursuit* of happiness. None of us are given any guarantee we

will actually achieve our goals. At least things are much easier for us today than in years past. Most of us (at least in the United States) do not spend our days trying to just survive (food, shelter, and clothing), although we may feel like it during the dark periods of our life. Ever want to test the theory? Go a day without electricity and running water—and I do not mean camping! I once hosted a foreign exchange student from Russia. At the time, I had a two-bedroom, one-bath condo. When she entered through the front door, she asked me, "How many families live with you?" Yikes. What a humbling moment and acknowledgement of how blessed we are in the United States of America. Somehow the consolation of knowing we are doing better than back in the day or than third-world or poor countries fails to comfort us during our valleys. All we know is, we hurt like hell.

⌘

One of my all-time favorite movies is *The Princess Bride*. Wesley, who is the acting Dread Pirate Roberts (you will have to watch it to appreciate the significance), finally confronts his true love, who is promised to be married to the king. He is not happy about the news and challenges her, although she does not know his real identity yet because she thinks he is dead. "Do not mock my pain," says Princess Buttercup, and Wesley snipes back, "Life is pain. Anyone who tells you differently is trying to sell you something." And so it is; we struggle. Some of us learn lessons fairly quickly, while others take a little longer to get it. The saying goes, "A wise man learns from his mistakes, but a wiser man learns from the mistakes of others." Suffice to say I have not always been wise at all. I seem to be the sort who needs to get hit over the head several times with the frying pan before I get the point. I suspect I am not the only one, especially with matters of the heart.

*The state of your life is nothing more than
a reflection of your state of mind.*
~ WAYNE DYER ~
American philosopher

Thankfully, I know all my hardships, whether internally or externally imposed, have a purpose. I also believe good can come from even the worst of circumstances. If the only positive outcome is I can share my experiences with others to help prevent them from falling into the same pits, I can accept my pain. However, God has done much, much more with my hurts and wounds, often allowing me to develop more compassion and less judgment of others. If we are willing, the tough times can teach us invaluable lessons about faith, trust, hope, and peace.

I would like to say my challenges have made me immune to repeat offenses, but alas, I am not perfect. Perhaps I have more growing to do in certain areas, and the hiccups of life provide an excellent opportunity for me to improve. I choose to embrace what comes my way and trust it all works together for my greater good.

Life Certainly Isn't Perfect

The trouble with our valleys is when we are in them, we often cannot see the lush green meadows ahead of us. We also tend to forget the cool springs we left behind. We get so entrapped by our circumstances that all we see is dry, desolate, cracked, decayed, and broken ground. We are parched, and our thirst consumes us.

My desert started on the night of my thirteenth birthday when my father died. He suffered incredible amounts of pain to avoid dying on my actual birthday, but he did not make it. The nurses, who took a liking to his kind and funny spirit, honored his final wish, though, and marked the death certificate *12:02 a.m. October 2, 1979*—the day *after* my birthday.

I will never forget my mother coming in late that night. I knew something was wrong and got up. She looked me in the eye and said, "It's all over." My daddy was gone forever, and I was left wondering what happened and how God could let this happen.

My mom, grief stricken, retreated into herself and became a cold, critical, and controlling monster. I spent my teen years trying to avoid her wrath and keep the peace at any cost. The price I paid was my own happiness—then and in the future.

Because I lacked support, encouragement, and love, I had a horrible self-image. I believed I was unworthy of love. As a result, I dated the most wretched men. The more selfish, dysfunctional, deficient, and abusive the man was, the greater the attraction for me. At the time, I could never understand why I did not like nice boys. I now know I felt I didn't deserve anything better than a loser. My mom set the standard: cruel mistreatment, conditional love, and withholding of acceptance.

In my past relationships, I have been beaten to the point where my organs have swollen up three times their size. I have been strangled blue and near death, slammed into walls, and called the most unpleasant, hurtful things. The physical torture was easier to overcome, but the messages I was ugly, fat, and unlovable took longer to heal—*much* longer. In essence, the men in my life continued the emotional abuse I received from my mother, and the churches I attended built upon that foundation: I was unworthy and vile. When I finally got the courage to seek divorce, my church family told me I would burn in hell. I was not permitted to rid my life of my evil, abusive husband; I was told to just live with it.

So you understand something about me: I am a very strong, determined, disciplined, and successful business woman. I broke corporate records for getting to the management level at a young age, and I did it in a male-dominated industry. I won awards and racked up professional achievements, certifications, and made great money. The problem was I had no concept of a healthy relationship. My heart desperately sought what I truly desired, but my subconscious found what was familiar. Red flags would go up left and right, but I did not have the self-worth to stand up for myself, and I certainly didn't have anyone fighting on my behalf. At one point, a close relative told me to marry an uneducated bald man because I probably couldn't do any better. I stumbled from one bad relationship to another, getting further away from what I really wanted and deserved.

Life Can Knock You Down

Because I was climbing the corporate ladder fast and furious, weeks turned into months, and months into years. I accepted, tolerated, and settled for a miserable home life. Everything had to come crashing down all at once for me to finally get it. Then and only then was I able to recognize my destructive pattern of aligning myself with unhealthy men. I will save you all the gory details, but I was unemployed as I went through a bitter divorce and the death of my mother at the same time. Finally separating meant a move back home, except I did not have one—or a car or many possessions. Oh yeah, I did not have any money either; he took that, too.

I fell and fell hard. I dropped down to 97 pounds at nearly five feet, ten inches and fought bouts of bronchitis and pneumonia. My body was slowly dying, and my spirit was beaten down. God's strength became very real for me, and He placed some dear and loving people in my life to walk my journey with me.

Thankfully, my mother and I had worked through our issues some six years prior to her death. Through lots of tears, we saw each other's perspectives and owned our contribution. My mom realized she was not a mother at all to me after my dad's death. She was unable to deal with the grief *and* raising a child. As a result, she treated me like an adult and expected me to behave accordingly. Her remorse and apology certainly did not erase the negative messages I heard during those most critical years of my development, but they healed us enough to allow us to move forward and create a *new* relationship. She was easier going and less critical; I let go of my resentment and bitterness. We had a great six years together, talking every day and laughing often. What a blessing! Though short, this time helped me understand the strengths and good things I received from my mom—and I would most certainly need them!

One trait I inherited was a positive attitude. When my mom was diagnosed with her terminal brain tumor, she knew God could heal her, but she was okay if He chose not to. She spent the last months of her life loving all of us through our pain and ensuring everyone was in a good place. I was homeless, unemployed, and broke as I went through my divorce, yet I truly was in a better place. I was free from the bondage, torment, and hellacious relationship with my ex. Mom and I agreed her illness got me out of a terrible situation, and it was a very good thing. I would soon realize I needed more than a positive outlook to get back up; I would need courage as I later faced two incurable diseases.

> *We gain strength and courage and confidence*
> *in each experience in which we stop to look fear in the face. …*
> *We must do that which we think we cannot.*
> ~ Anna Eleanor Roosevelt ~
> *Former First Lady*

Life as We Know It

Mom died in May, and my divorce was final in July. I moved away from my hometown and started my own business in August with only $500 to my name, which I got from her final settlement. Although my eyes were open to my poor judgment and mistakes I had made with men, I would spend years understanding the layers of toxicity I allowed in my life with work, friends, and family. I was angry not just at my ex for all the horrendous things he said and did, but I was mad at myself for allowing such garbage in my life. *How did I get here?* kept gnawing at me. Not one to get stuck in anger or blaming others, I quickly turned to the one person who was ultimately responsible for my hardship: me.

The reality is I have spent my entire life trying to save others. I thought I could love people out of their dysfunctions and inspire them to be better people. The painful truth is, most people don't want to change, and even if they did, I cannot do the work for them. I have dedicated so much energy to learning what matters to everyone else that I still have to pause when asked, "What would *you* like?" I sincerely don't know some times. I have so many voices in my head—my mother's negative control, my ex's abuse, one-sided relationships with friends, my family's self-centeredness, and the church's twisted adaptation of God's Word—that I still need some time to quiet them all and listen for my small whisper. I am getting better at hearing my own voice, but I must continually work at it. What I learned is we all train people on how to treat us.

We train people on how to treat us.

What we tolerate is what we get. Understanding why we tolerate what we do is the key, and I am still working through the layers. Toxic relationships come in all sizes and shapes. I had friends dump me after my divorce because they could not hang around such a sinner. I have had family say I just didn't deserve any better, so just settle for a loser. I have even been sexually harassed and discriminated against by Christian companies. Again, I permitted these people to treat me poorly because I believed at some level I deserved it.

The turning point for any us comes when we have finally had

enough. We are sick of ending up in the same place. After countless vampiric friends, disappointment with my family's behavior, abusive men, and frustrating business situations, I decided I needed to change. Someone famously quipped, "Insanity is doing the same things over and over again and expecting different results." Attempting to change everyone else was my insanity, and it was exhausting.

If you are frustrated, disappointed, and discouraged, then stop allowing toxins into your life. If you are wondering how you ended up here or how you can restart your life, then read on!

As for me, my new business boomed immediately. I had clients across the country and was making more money than ever before. Then, my move to a new town led me to the love of my life—a real man with passion, heart, and soul. I had a new life!

A New Life

A new life awaits you as well. The sooner you understand you are not the cause of others' problems and you cannot, therefore, cure them, you will be on your way to establishing healthier relationships. When you can maturely respond to tough situations rather than reacting, you will no longer be powerless in your own life. Creating new patterns takes work. We must not only remove the toxins, but we must replace them with something positive. God's truth is a wonderful tool. If you ever doubt your value, just read God's words. They are for you!

Life is a gift from God.
What we do with it is our gift back to Him.
~ ANONYMOUS ~

Although I am very thankful for meeting my soul mate, marrying a wonderful man doesn't make your relationship immune from hardship. We were newlyweds and had just bought our first home when my five-year contract was broken. My husband had given up his occupation as a commercial fishing captain, as it was impossible to do that job and be married when he would be gone for eight to nine months at a time. We found ourselves in a new town with a mortgage and no income. Shortly after that, I began to get sick, which you'll read more about later.

As I write this, we are celebrating 21 years of marriage. We've been through and come through a lot. We've remained partners, friends, and lovers through all the ups and downs. Once again, we are facing yet another difficult time, and I know this is my opportunity to apply my own FIT Life principles and affirm my resolve and renew my faith. My prayer has been to have peace through the storm, keep my eyes up while in the valley, and trust God for our future.

Wherever you are in life, trials will come. Besides paying taxes and dying, we can count on this to be true! I would love to say lessons learned in years past will not be repeated, but I would be lying. I am, after all, the one who needs repeated head hitting with a frying pan to get the point. What I can promise you is this: God is WAY bigger than anything tossed at us. His strength is sufficient, and I can personally attest to that. It is real.

My wish for you is that you might be brave in times of trial. When others lay crosses upon your shoulders, or when mountains must be climbed and chasms to be crossed or when hope can scare shine through … that every gift God gave you might grow along with you. That you may always have a friend who is worth that name whom you can trust, and who helps you in times of sadness … who will defy the storms of daily life at your side. One more wish I have for you: that every hour of joy and pain, you may feel God close to you.
~ IRISH BLESSING ~

May the stories shared in this book remind you that you are not alone! Your mistakes may be different, but they are no worse than anything here. You will not receive judgment but rather understanding, support, encouragement, hope, and inspiration to once and for all say ENOUGH! You can and *will* get back up when life knocks *you* down. If even only one story impacts you and influences your life for the better, then I consider it a victory.

I believe in you and will be cheering you on during your journey. Keep the faith, defy your diagnosis, and get YOUR life back today!

DEFY YOUR DIAGNOSIS INTRODUCTION

FIT Life Formula @ Work

On a scale of 1 to 10, how close are you to God right now? Explain.

On a scale of 1 to 10, how good are you at trusting God through the tough times? Explain.

Why did you pick up this book?

What has knocked you down?

Have you reached your tipping point? If so, share it.

CHAPTER ONE

Time For A Shift with the FIT Life Formula!

You must make a choice to take a chance
if you want anything in life to change.
~ ANONYMOUS ~

I don't know what kind of year you have had, but mine has been incredibly challenging. In fact, the last two and a half have been flat-out tough. I know I'm not alone as I hear countless stories of financial struggle, emotional heartache, illness, disappointment, and discouragement. This is NOT how we are supposed to be living!

I believe a shift is required. However, most of us are waiting for God to shift things for us when we must be actively involved. Remember the story from Joshua in the Bible of the men carrying the ark of the covenant? When they approached the Jordan River, its waters were too deep and its flow too strong to cross. They asked God to part the waters so they could cross, but He denied their request. At the time, this probably felt like a punishment, but God had other plans. He told them they must first step in to the river deep to display their trust in Him. Then and only then would He part the waters. When they took a step of faith, they were protected and blessed … and their faith grew.

The lesson for us is that we must pursue and move toward what we feel God wants for us; we cannot sit on the sidelines and wait. No one benefits from us passively waiting. Those looking at our Christian walk won't want anything to do with our God if all they see is stagnant situations riddled with pain and suffering, and we will most certainly feel defeated. We will be left wondering where God is and why He hasn't answered our prayers, when in fact, He has already provided everything for us—we simply need to go get it! We have to take a step of faith before He will pour His abundance upon us.

Here's the visual I received during my prayer time:

Picture Mount Everest. This mountain of a climb cannot be done all at once but rather has stages to complete. Base camps are set up to offer temporary rest and reprieve from the hard journey. These camps were never designed with comfort in mind; they are primitive and only provide the basic essentials of shelter. They are intended to help people move forward to the ultimate goal: the summit! They aren't the destination.

I can only speak for myself, but I am stuck at the base camp. Instead of catching my breath, I have built a structure here. It is bleak, uncomfortable, and I am suffering as a result. I have looked to the heavens wondering, *Why I am here?* But I stayed put. My suffering is my own making. Because I was weary, I doubted; my doubt led to fear; and I allowed my feelings of despair to consume me. And yes, Satan has had a part! He has been whispering in my ear that this IS as good as it gets *for me*. This is all I am worth, and I shouldn't hope or expect for more.

As a coach and inspirational speaker, I uplift countless people. I'm a prayer warrior for my friends and family. I have absolute confidence that their prayers will be answered. Sitting at this cold, desolate camp I'd created, I realized I hadn't believed God's Word and promises for me. In order for a true shift to occur for me so that I could receive all God has for me, I had to break free of my own bondage; I had leave base camp. I could no longer believe it is right for things to be wrong for me.

Have you prayed until you have no words left or cried a river of tears? Please continue reading. God has words of encouragement, and I want to share them with you.

♋

I love driving cars with gear shifts. Manual gear shifts give you more control of your speed and keep you engaged in the process. The smarter cars get, the dumber we seem to be on the roads! I think we are checking out and not actively participating (besides texting and driving, which is an entirely different conversation for another day).

For the same reason, if we truly want to experience a shift in our life, we will need to take some action.

- **S**top Believing Satan's Lies

- **H**old on to God's Promises

- **I**gnite Your Dreams

- **F**lee Your Past

- **T**ake What God Has for You!

As I make shifts in my own life, I hope you will join me. Be brave, bold, and believe!

Stop Believing Satan's Lies

Satan never enters our life through the front door; instead, he sneaks in the back door in the dark of night. He is a tiny whisper in desperate times, and he seeks to plant seeds of doubt within us. That is all he needs to do, because we do the rest. We water those seeds and make sure they get plenty of sunshine. We talk to them and ever fertilize them regularly.

Satan is also clever. His lies never look the same. Oh, the intent and ultimate message are the same, but they take different shapes. He is a master at shape-shifting his lies so that we do not recognize them. One day they look like dragons, so we avoid dragons, but the problem is he shape-shifted again. Now his lies are ogres, and we are caught off guard since we were keeping an eye out for dragons. This is how he sneaks up on us without warning, and we are struggling once again with our self-worth.

No matter how much church I attended, I still didn't believe I was loved and worthy of good things. My head knew God's Word, but my heart resisted the message. If we truly accepted and embraced God's love for us, Satan would have no stronghold against us. His lies would repel off our godly armor and fall flat on the ground. The common denominator in all my broken relationships is me.

Part of our godly armor is discerning the different voices we hear. I'm not talking about your parent's voice or that of a spouse that rattles around and influences your decisions. No, I'm talking about spiritual voices that guide us. The four spiritual voices I have identified are: God's, our soul's, our spirit's, and Satan's.

You may not have studied the difference between our soul and our spirit, but I encourage you to do so, because it is fascinating and makes incredible sense to me. Our soul is where our history lies. It is what makes us who we are; it is our imprint. Everything that makes us unique resides here—including all our mistakes. Our soul is very protective and acts like our best friend (think Jesus). It's a voice of reason. However, it can also be overprotective and not permit us to take that leap of faith required.

Our spirit is connected straight to the source of light through the Holy Spirit—God in us. It is much more adventurous and has no fear. Our spirit has seen the master plan and knows that we will fulfill our destiny. Unfortunately, it can leap without looking.

That's where God's voice comes in. He leads our soul and spirit in the right direction. He ensures that everyone is working together. But the challenge is, His voice is the quietest. He isn't going to shout to get our attention. We must quiet our minds and intently listen.

Satan can certainly talk the loudest at times to distract us and consume our minds with the wrong things, like stress. When we worry, we aren't focusing on God's Word or promises. We cannot have both lies and truth residing together. One cancels out the other just like light consumes the darkness. Satan can also whisper what appears to be harmless thoughts when in reality, they trick us falling away from God.

Like anything, practice is required. It takes discipline to discern between the voices. Pay attention to how you feel when a voice comes. Do you sweat? Does your stomach hurt? Your body will give away signs long before it registers in your mind. Check in with the Father. Seek Him out and ask for clarity. The good news is, the odds are in our favor three to one! They key to denying and rebuking Satan's lies is to know God and His Word.

"The thief comes only to steal and kill and destroy;
I have come that they may have life, and have it to the full."
~ JOHN 10:10 ~

Hold on to God's Promises

The Bible is full of hope. Have you read it lately? I mean, have you really read it and allowed the messages of truth, hope, and love penetrate your very being? I am guilty of getting into a rut and not putting enough importance on this powerful book. Life gets busy, and we get consumed with activity. However, everything we need is found in that book. Each time we read it, we breathe life into God's message for us.

Weak? God can help you be strong.

Afraid? God will give you courage.

Lost? God will offer guidance.

Feeling alone? God loves you!

With thousands of promises from our heavenly Father, why then do we doubt? How can we doubt we are loved for even a nanosecond? The answer is, we are human. God did not make us robots and that means we will have human emotions. God wants us to choose Him and follow Him because we want to, not because He demanded it.

Nothing we are facing is above or beyond God's reach, but we must have faith. We must hold on to His promises found in the Bible and placed upon our hearts. He speaks to each of us differently and places specific promises inside of us. Our job is to fan the flame and keep it burning until we see our prayers answered in His perfect timing.

If you have been a Christian for any length of time, you understand that God's timing is not ours. What often feels like 11:55 to us is just perfect to Him. As you trust and hold on to God's promises, remain steadfast with your faith. Cling to His words and offer up prayers of praise and gratitude for all He has already done in your life. He is working behind the scenes right now to deliver your answer. We must be ready and willing to accept His blessings.

Sometimes our abundance gets delayed because our faith stalled, like my story of the Everest base camp. Take a spiritual inventory to determine how you are doing. Ask God to forgive for doubting and ask Him to restore your faith. With Him, all things are possible!

"'For I know the plans I have for you,' says the Lord, 'plans to prosper
you and not to harm you, plans to give you hope and a future.'"
~ JEREMIAH 29:11 ~

Ignite Your Dreams

Depending upon how last year went for you, you might have given up on your dreams. I hope not, but I understand discouragement. As a goal-oriented individual, I can get quite focused on what I want to accomplish. I think we are all guilty of holding so tightly to a dream that we can't admit when it has died. And yes, dreams do die. Sometimes, we didn't take the dream seriously, and thus it withered from lack of water. We outgrow some dreams. What we thought we wanted when we were in our teens may change through the years. Other times, despite our best efforts, life throws a curve ball, and our dream is stepped on, crushed in its infant stages. We are brought to our knees, crying out, "Now what?"

Like any death, we need to bury it and pay respects. Honor your dead dream, but do not hold on to it. When we don't let go of the dead, we can never move on. I believe we must grieve and mourn the loss of our beloved dream. Then, we must let it go so another dream can live! Yes, new dreams are awaiting you. You just didn't see them or acknowledge them because you were stuck with your old, dead dream. Start watering your new dream today. Give it energy, and watch it blossom! When one dream dies, don't lose all hope. Room is created for new dreams, and they may just surprise you.

God has plans for you, and it is time to dream again. Answer these questions to help you narrow down what your new dream might look like:

- What do you want MORE of this year?

- What do you want LESS of this year?

- What's the biggest mistake you made last year?

- Are there tasks/things that are wasting your time and talents?

- Did certain things frustrate you over and over again?

- What did you do last year that brought you joy?

- What relationships (personal and professional) do you need to nurture more?

- What are you most curious about that you haven't taken the time to learn?

- What three words best describe last year?

• What words do you want to describe this year?

If you are discouraged, have faith! If you have no idea how things will work out, trust. When we are in the darkest of places, deep in the tunnel, God comes to meet us with His light and shows the way. When circumstances truly seem impossible is when God says, *Now let me show you what I can do!*

Flee Your Past

Ever feel like your past keeps finding you? Chances are you put your hurts and wounds in a small trailer, and you have been towing them around. They remain locked up, but they are always with you. At first, the load was light, but as the years have gone, the drag is slowing you down. In some cases (like me), you may have come to a complete stop.

All the counseling and self-help books (including this booklet) won't erase your past. We can't change what happened; however, we can choose to learn from it and let it go. Easier said than done! Just when we think something we said or done in the past isn't influencing today, we find ourselves in the same place. We are running a pattern, and until we decide to behave differently, we will be stuck in a loop of bondage. To break this bondage, we have to leave the camp. Don't take your time and gather your things—RUN! God wants us to show our faith and pursue Him with gusto. Just like when he healed the paralyzed man: Go! Walk! He didn't tell the man to first crawl and try it out. No, He commanded full participation.

To truly flee our past and be free once and for all, I believe we need to:

➤ Forgive ourselves and others

➤ Receive God's message and direction

➤ Embrace our situations and circumstances

➤ Emulate the truth

Take What God Has for You

God is waiting for you. He has already provided everything you need. He's heard your prayers and has answered them. You simply need to believe it and run toward it. Look for His outstretched hand and muster up the strength, faith, and courage to grab it tight. Claim: This is mine! *I am worthy of His abundance—not because of how great I **am** but because my God is so great!*

TIME FOR A SHIFT

A new chapter awaits you, but only you can close the old chapter. You must know in every fiber of your being that the conditions of hardship, strain, frustration, disappointment, grief, sadness, loneliness, and financial poverty are over.

God awaits your arrival. He has already provided ALL you have asked and has huge blessings for you. You must simply run toward Him. Seek Him out; He will show you the way. He will not make you leave base camp, and He cannot stop you from listening to deceitful lies. You must choose Him and reach for His hand. We must live out the FIT Life Formula: A foundation in Faith, continually Insights into Personal Development, and keep Tackling the Tough Stuff!

I hope you will muster up the strength and faith to grab ahold of what truly is yours: abundance. A new chapter begins only when you close the old one.

It truly is a time for a SHIFT. Will you dare make it? If you do, let it be a season of …

- Refilling your bank account and repaying all that has been financially lost

- Reigniting your passion for life, love, and Him

- Renewing your marriage with trust, honor, and respect

- Reclaiming your dreams

- Restarting those opportunities that once stalled

- Restoring your health to one of vitality

- Reenergizing your relationships

- Rebuilding the right business connections

- Reorganizing your thoughts to align with His

- Reevaluating emotions and erasing old, destructive messages

- Redeeming your spirit in the Lord Jesus Christ

A SHIFT comes when we decide to run away from what we have created and run toward what God has designed for us. Don't worry about what direction or where—just run. As I visualize myself running away from my camp of bondage, I cannot see exactly where I am going. Yet I know God will be my guide. His light will lead me, and His voice will encourage me. His abundance awaits me, and it awaits you!

I'm here to guide you on the journey, and God is with you.

DEFY YOUR DIAGNOSIS CHAPTER ONE

FIT Life Formula @ Work

Thinking of last's years struggles, which ones were self-created?

What difficulties were placed upon you by someone else?

What just happened?

What SHIFT do you need to make for a better year ahead?

What one thing are you seeking God and asking Him to deliver?

CHAPTER TWO

Fight To Get Your Life Back!

When in the world are we going to begin to live as
if we understood that this is life? This is our time, our day
... and it is passing. What are we waiting for?
~ RICHARD L. EVANS ~
Writer

"I'll start exercising when the kids are older."

"I'll start concentrating on 'me' after work slows down."

"I've just got too much on my plate."

"I just need to get past this busy season."

The list goes on. As a former personal trainer and life coach, I have heard countless statements from people, especially women, that lead me to believe we really don't understand that this is our life, and we do not get a second chance.

Perhaps you have caught yourself making one of these statements. I completely understand; in fact, I've made them myself. It simply means you are human! But you can do something about it, which is why I'm glad that you have picked up this book.

Life is much more complicated than in years gone by, and as women, we have double the workload. I recently attended a workshop where we were asked to name the different "hats" we wear on a given day. As I started labeling my hats, I realized that women really are expected to be many things to many people. Here is what my list looks like:

- Child of God
- Wife
- Best friend
- Friend
- Sister
- Cousin
- Aunt
- Great Aunt
- Daughter-in-law
- Neighbor
- Pet owner
- Business owner
- Speaker
- Trainer
- Executive coach
- Fitness instructor
- Life coach
- Mentor
- Facilitator
- Writer
- Author
- Leader
- Community leader

I might be missing a hat or two, but even so, it's certainly a big list—even overwhelming. Why don't you make your own list?

- _____
- _____
- _____
- _____
- _____
- _____
- _____
- _____
- _____

- _____
- _____
- _____
- _____
- _____
- _____
- _____

I am sure your list will be just as long, if not longer, especially if you have children. The list will give you a good idea of the many different directions you are being pulled and the amount of energy you are expending. I know you may be stressed out and feeling the ramifications of wearing many hats. Statistics tell us we all are.

Totally out of Control

The National Mental Health Association reports that 75–95 percent of all visits to the doctor are stress related. Over half the population is overweight, and 80 percent of us suffer from back pain. One million Americans have heart attacks each year, and eight million have stomach ulcers. Stress can also cause the following:

➤ Low energy

➤ Restless nights and lack of sleep

➤ Digestive problems

➤ Memory impairment

➤ Depression or anxiety

➤ Decreased productivity

➤ Unhappiness

➤ Frequent illness

➢ Low sex drive

➢ Serious illness

Are you experiencing any of the symptoms on that list? Stress may be to blame. Even if your stress is work-related, it can negatively affect your personal life … and vice versa. Unfortunately, our best attempts to segment our stress don't really work; stress *will* follow us. Marital problems, financial worries, even your troubled teens will come to work with you. Similarly, pressing deadlines, a mean boss, and unco-operative co-workers will come home with you at the end of the day. It's no wonder we don't feel good. Here's a fact, ladies: If we aren't doing something with our stress, it is doing something to us. We can-not passively sit by and let stress destroy our lives. We need to get our lives back!

> *Most folks are about as happy as they make up their mind to be.*
> ~ ABRAHAM LINCOLN ~
> *Former president of the United States*

I was asked to speak to a group of Girl Scouts on the topic of stress. When I asked the girls, ages ten to twelve, to define stress for me, one girl replied, "It's a headache." Another girl offered, "It's a stomach-ache." Then a girl in the back yelled, "It's when I kick the dog!" Even our children understand what stress feels like! But what exactly is it?

What Exactly Is Stress?

Stress is a small word that packs a powerful punch. Personally, I believe it is responsible for most ailments, fatigue, missed deadlines, and dissatisfaction in our lives. Stress, in a nutshell, is a chemical reaction to the wear and tear on your body caused by life's events, as defined by Dr. Hans Seyle. Our adrenal glands pump, our blood pres-sure rises, and our cortisol levels increase. Cortisol is a stress hormone that increases sugar (glucose) in the bloodstream and alters our immune system response. Cortisol is known to interfere with weight loss, and it causes inflammation in our system, which is attributed to many of the autoimmune disorders. You've heard the expression "fight or flight," right? It refers to our body's ability to shift into high gear in times of trouble. It was useful in prehistoric times when we needed to run away from a wild animal, but it can cause problems in our civilized world. With the pace of life we are living now, our bodies are constantly trying to run away. We are stuck in fight mode. We may not have wild animals chasing us, but stress is around every corner. People, events, and media messages bombard us. Sometimes we may feel we are on a treadmill with the speed stuck on high. Help!

> *Unhappiness is not knowing what we want*
> *and killing ourselves to get it.*
> ~ DON HEROLD ~
> *American humorist*

Different Types of Stress

In order to better understand stress, I like to break it down into three types: negative stress, positive stress, and motivating stress.

1. We are quite familiar with *negative stress*. We feel it during difficult times of life, such as when we experience death, divorce, or loss of job. During such times, we know we are under duress and can feel the effects physically, mentally, emotionally, and spiritually.

2. What some of us don't realize is that we experience stress even in the happy times of life, such as getting married, having a baby, or moving into a new house. Although these are wonderful moments, they come with what I call *positive stress*. Anyone who

has planned a wedding understands this all too well. It is one of the most exciting times of your life, and yet you are stressed out by the endless details and family dynamics. The pressure is on for you to make this the most spectacular and perfect event. That is what I call stress. Here's the kicker: Our bodies do not distinguish between the two; the same chemical reaction takes place.

Whether feeling negative or positive stress,
our body's chemical reaction is the same.
~ Dr. Hans Seyle ~
American Stress Institute

3. Last is *motivating stress,* which allows us to get to work on time, meet deadlines, and get things done. I also use the term "life pressures." Alarm clocks, calendars, schedules, to-do lists … they all serve a purpose for us, but they create some stress. Without them, however, we wouldn't function nearly as efficiently, and that would cause another kind of stress altogether. As a writer, I am given a deadline for my article or manuscript, along with guidelines regarding the length. Motivating stress helps me to complete it on time and as promised. Could I write without a due date? Yes, but having the pressures keeps me on target and helps prevent procrastination. We all need those little nudges in life.

Are you a runner? I'm certainly not a die-hard runner—those folks who run at a good clip for ten miles at a pop. I'm more into three-to-five-mile runs at a leisurely pace. Nevertheless, one day I was out running at warp speed. I amazed myself, actually. I was breaking every record I had for that particular loop. I even began thinking of signing up for a marathon *until* I turned around. I realized I had been running *with* the wind (positive stress). Once I had to run against the wind, I could barely move (negative stress). My motivating stress became, *Just get home!* Stress is in every aspect of our lives.

No Such Thing as Stress-Free

As much as we would like to believe commercials, ads, and promises for a life of complete peace and tranquility, we will never live a life with zero stress. Somehow, we do need to realize that today is the only day of its kind we will experience. Yesterday is already in the past. We do not have the opportunity to relive it. What happened or didn't happen is already a memory. We need to concentrate on the here and now. Unfortunately, as a society we have fallen into the trap of virtually sleepwalking through our lives. Then we wake up some morning wondering, *What in the world happened to me?* I hear it from women every day.

It Sneaks Up on Us

A client came in to see me for an assessment of her physical condition. On the telephone, she mentioned she might be a few pounds overweight. When she came to my studio, she told me she had gotten out of the habit of exercising. Her work schedule was extremely busy, and before she knew it, her life got out of balance. She was spending most of her time at work and very little time on things she enjoyed.

I always like to get benchmarks for my clients, so we measured her and determined her body fat percentage. When I reviewed the numbers with her, she turned white and began to cry. She was confronted finally with reality: She was obese. She was 80 pounds overweight, with over 50 percent of her body consisting of fat—the red zone for heart disease and other ailments. All she could say was, "How did this happen?" Well, days had turned into weeks, weeks into months, and months eventually into years. Now she found herself in a place she didn't like, and she had to get herself out. The good news is that she took the first step, and we began to look at how she was handling stress.

You need to do the same thing. And like my client, you'll find that taking small steps will make a huge difference.

Don't forget until it's too late that the business
of life is not business, but living.
~ B. C. FORBES ~
Journalist

Stress Reactions

I don't know about you, but my parents never told me about any of this. I had to figure it out on my own, thus my crash and burn when the stuff hit the fan. As a result, most of us end up with our own ways of dealing with stress. Some of us work our way through it, while others drink ourselves numb. The unhealthy ways of dealing with stress seem easy to find:

- Overeating
- Undereating
- Alcoholism
- Misuse of legal and illegal drugs
- Smoking
- Emotional outbursts
- Control issues
- Anger
- "Workaholism"
- Withdrawal and isolation

- Excessive sleeping

- Depression

How are you currently managing your stress? Is it working? Think of others you encounter in your life: How are they coping?

ʘ

The other day I ran to the office supply store. Two registers were open, and one had no line. The other register had a customer ringing up and a lady waiting. Since the lady was there first, I asked, "Do you want to check out at the other register since no one is waiting?" She proceeded to bite my head off, barking, "I will check out wherever I like, and you have to wait on my decision!" Okay! I guess I was the straw that broke her back. I proceeded to check out at the other register.

As a society, we are wound up way too tight and living on the edge. That's the reason for this book: to help you take steps in all areas of your life to bring balance … to regain your life, one piece at a time! In order to do that, we must be honest with ourselves. How did we end up here? What is stress costing us?

Turning Points

For me, it was a major crisis that forced me to evaluate my life. I had just turned thirty and had been transferred to England with my then-husband, who was in the U.S. Air Force. I was in an abusive marriage but had chosen to suffer silently. You know, *I made my bed, and now I need to sleep in it.* That was how I was raised.

Besides the ongoing stress of our relationship, I had the stress of leaving my family and friends and quitting my own career to make the move. I did what I always do to cope: I got involved, figuring that if I stayed busy, I wouldn't have time to think. If I didn't have time to think, then I couldn't feel anything. And if I couldn't feel anything, I wouldn't hurt. Ever think that way? That's what I call "stinking thinking"!

Anyway, I volunteered at the church, taught fitness classes, and began substitute teaching in the American schools. I felt I was doing okay, until my mother came to visit for Christmas. When she got off the plane, she didn't know who I was, and half of her face was paralyzed. My world came to a screeching halt. She was quickly diagnosed with an inoperable, terminal brain tumor. I needed to get her back to the States. My husband threatened to divorce me if I left to help her. That was my defining moment. I left England and never went back.

In five short months, I watched my mother die before my eyes. She and I had had our problems, but I loved her deeply. During that same time period, I went through a painful divorce. However, I was expending so much energy to love my mother through her last days that none of that mattered. What I didn't realize is that I wasn't managing all of the stress well at all. Finally, one day shortly after my mother's funeral, I could barely get out of bed. I had dropped down to 97 pounds, at nearly five feet, ten inches tall. I had lost so much muscle that my body could barely function; it had started to shut down. That was my turning point. I knew I had to manage stress better, or it truly would kill me.

I needed to get *my* life back.

The Silent Killer

You may be hurting. You may be exhausted, overwhelmed, and feeling completely out of control. You may doubt whether you can ever get your life back, but I am here to tell you that you can! You can overcome your challenges, big or small, and create a healthier life for yourself and your loved ones. I encourage you to commit to changing your life, step by step. In this book I will try to help you with ideas, tips, and suggestions, so you don't feel like the woman who left this note:

If I'm not here, I'm lost.
I've gone to look for myself.
If I should return before I get back,
Please have me wait until I return.
~ ANONYMOUS ~

Ten short years after my turning point, I took a cruise with my new husband, who truly is a gift from God, to celebrate my big 4-0 birthday. As I reflected on all that had transpired in my life, I was extremely grateful I learned healthier ways to manage my stress. It did not kill me, and with God's help, I survived and conquered. I had rebuilt my career, created a happier marriage, and restored my body by exercising and eating right. God truly blessed me and continues to bless me. Friends, don't lose hope. A new life is possible!

Trust in the LORD with all your heart
and lean not on your own understanding;
in all your ways submit to him,
and he will make your paths straight.
~ PROVERBS 3:5–6 ~

DEFY YOUR DIAGNOSIS CHAPTER TWO

FIT Life Formula @ Work

How are you currently managing your stress?

Is it working?

What one negative response to stress do you want to eliminate?

Why?

What will you do instead when stressed?

CHAPTER THREE

Manage Your Time

"Better three hours too soon, than one minute too late."
~ WILLIAM SHAKESPEARE ~
English poet

Ticktock. Ticktock. Time is certainly ticking away. Wherever you are, a clock is clicking away the minutes. Another one just went by as you read this sentence. Time waits for no man (or woman) and keeps marching on.

In order to help you get some of your life back, we must look at how you manage your time. Are you organized? Do you keep a tidy house, everything in its place? Are you a master of scheduling and planning? Or are you like many women I know: constantly running late, forgetting appointments, never quite getting to everything you need to do, and feeling frustrated?

Many clients have come to me in sheer desperation, their lives utterly out of control and their stress levels at the max. Unfortunately, a lifetime of hearing people say, "Do what feels good; you are okay and I am okay" deceived us into believing that we didn't have to do certain hard things, like manage our time. One client rebelled against my suggestions, saying they would confine her, restrict her creativity, and make her unhappy. Well, she was already miserable; what did she have to lose? The reality of getting your life organized is that you *will* have more free time and less stress. This, in turn, will allow you to have extra creativity and joy. Interested?

It Takes Commitment

Let me ask you this before we go any further: What would you do with an extra thirty minutes? I actually want you to write it down here, so please take a moment to think about it and respond.

_____

_____

_____

_____

_____

_____

_____

_____

No answer is wrong. This is *your* extra thirty minutes. Would you sleep? Exercise? Play with the kids? Visit family? Work? Read? By managing your time better, you can easily gain thirty minutes every day! Use what you wrote as motivation to apply the principles in this book.

Want to get really serious? Then fill in and sign the success contract below. I have every coaching and fitness client sign one. Although the contract is not legally binding, it puts on paper your commitment and your promise to do the work. If you want to get the most out of this book, I encourage you to fill this out and have a loved one or trusted friend sign as your accountability partner. I'll be your coach!

Success Contract

I, _____, hereby make a commitment to read this book with the intent of changing my time management, thoughts, emotions, physical condition, relationships, and spiritual life. I do want my life back!

I agree to try and apply the principles, tips, and suggestions in this book for at least thirty days.

When I have kept this agreement, I believe and trust that I will be a healthier and happier person. I will celebrate by _____

_____

_____

_____

_____

Signature: _____

Date: _____

Witness: _____

Date: _____

I always include a place to spell out what you will do when you succeed, because I firmly believe that we need to celebrate our victories! Too often, especially in the workplace, we move from one goal or achievement to the next without pausing long enough to say, "Good job" or "Well done!" I won't lie to you; getting your life back will take some work, because it took a while to get out of balance. The good news is that it won't take nearly as long to get it back into shape.

One of the most surprising things for clients who come to me to lose weight is how quickly they can get to a healthy weight. Oftentimes, years and years of doing the wrong things and not doing the right things gets a person overweight, but in a matter of months, a person can get to a good weight. That's encouraging news, and so it is with your life. You will see improvements right away; it won't take you years to get more balanced … I promise.

> *It is no use saying, "We are doing our best."*
> *You have got to succeed in doing what is necessary.*
> ~ Sir Winston Churchill ~
> *Former British prime minister*

Event Management

This chapter is going to help you manage your time, although that is a misnomer of sorts, because we really can't control time at all. Time is what it is. Days are 24 hours long, weeks have 7 days, and the months turn into years, whether we like it or not. No matter what we do, we cannot slow down or speed up time. What we can do, however, is control the events in our lives; and after all, that's what life really is—a series of events. If we desire greater control and security, more order, and less stress, then we must manage the events that make up our lives. In this book, therefore, when we refer to or discuss time management, we are in essence addressing event management.

> *You don't get to choose how you're going to die … or when.*
> *You can only decide how you're going to live.*
> ~ Joan Baez ~
> *Singer*

The pages that follow describe time- and event-management techniques that can dramatically improve the quality of your life by helping you regain some control, order, and peace. By managing some of the "stuff" of our lives better, we can enjoy our lives more fully. As you read through, you may find that some of the tips and suggestions are habits for you already. Bravo! Others may be new to you, and I encourage you to give them a try.

> *If you do what you've always done,*
> *you'll get what you've always gotten.*
> ~ ANTHONY ROBBINS ~
> *Motivational speaker & author*

The First Step

When you read chapter 2, did you list all the hats you wear? Were you surprised at how much you have going on? Like me, you probably had been aware that you were busy but didn't realize how many different ways you were expending energy. Each of our hats has a multitude of events associated with it. When I coach people on managing their time and events more efficiently, one of the first things we do is to list those events and look at the cost associated with each of them. We know what we pay for gas and a gallon of milk, but most of us really don't have a clue about how much we pay for the events in our lives.

All events are not created equal. For instance, you will expend much more energy doing something you really don't want to do compared with something you enjoy. We'll address setting boundaries in the next chapter, but for now let's just say that without setting limits, you won't be in control.

Be deliberate with your life. Too often, we think that we have to say yes to everything. We feel obligated. We must change that mindset to one of evaluating what we do and determining what we see fit to do. I call it the Opportunity Scale.

The Opportunity Scale

Let me ask you this: As you are reading this book, what are you *not* doing? Some answers might be not doing the laundry, not sleeping, not working, and not feeding the dog. The truth is that as you read this book, you aren't doing *anything* else! By choosing to read it, you put a greater value on it at this moment than anything else. Thank you! I know you won't regret it if you stick with me.

On any given day or moment, opportunities present themselves to us. We have the choice to participate or not. And too often, my friend, that is what we have given up—our right to choose! Somewhere along the way, we just went along with life. Maybe as women we feel it is our duty. Well, ladies, it's time to get in the driver's seat!

Live as you will wish to have lived when you are dying.
~ CHRISTIAN FURCHTEGOT GELLERT ~
Poet

Think of opportunity in terms of a scale. When a choice comes along, weigh it against its cost.

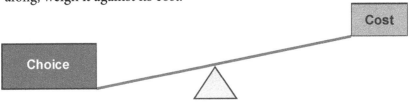

Choice

If the cost isn't too great, then you've made the right choice. If, on the other hand, the cost is too heavy, then you may want to reevaluate your decision. No right or wrong answers exist. I cannot tell you what to do, but I can tell you this: If you start being more consciously involved in your decision-making process, you will have less stress! As much as possible, make sure each opportunity outweighs the cost. This simple step will make a world of difference in your life! Start applying it immediately, okay?

The Secrets of Super Productive People

Now, back to those folks I briefly mentioned earlier—the ones you hate because they get everything done on time, are extremely organized, and seem to have it all together. What makes them so productive? Don't hate them; emulate them! You, too, can have a more organized life by using a system called IPPA. My husband and I developed it years ago, and ever since it has been helping folks get a handle on their lives. It is quite simple, really. IPPA stands for:

Identify what needs to be done.

Prioritize your goals and tasks in the order of their importance.

Plan when and how your goals and tasks will be achieved.

Act to achieve them.

In order for the system to work, you must pause long enough to look at the tasks and events in your life and determine what needs to be accomplished. Once you've done that, you can then prioritize the items, then plan and take action. Everyone is unique, so your process for doing this may be different from someone else's. Here's a selection of methods. See what works best for you.

- To-do list – A sheet of paper with your tasks listed. Down and dirty. Not fancy or formal.

- Planning sheet – Sheet of paper in a day planner that outlines your tasks and gives you ways of prioritizing them.

- Electronic device – Tablet, cell phone, BlackBerry, or other device that provides a means to keep your lists with you at all times.

- Sticky notes – Help you remember things on the fly.

- Goal list – A more formalized plan with specific details and due dates.

- Tickler file – A folder holding your to-do items in some order for you to retrieve.

- Calendar – A wall, pocket, or year-at-a-glance calendar offers daily and monthly tracking of events.

- Whiteboard – Write down or erase your to-do list as needed and keep it someplace visible.

- –Other – _____

I don't want you to get caught up in the "how" of doing it, as long as you accomplish the "what." The one method I would highly discourage you from using, though, is the "pile and bulldoze" method. This consists of stacking up piles until you can't find anything and then giving up, ultimately tossing everything and starting over. Some argue from among the piles that they know exactly where everything is, but I say hogwash! Folks, it has been proven over and over again that when the world around us is cluttered, so are our minds. And when our minds are cluttered, so is our soul. To reduce stress and regain some sanity, we need order. It will take some work, but you can do it!

No Pain, No Gain?

As a fitness professional, I don't always agree with the saying, "No pain, no gain." Exercising is work, but it shouldn't hurt to the point of being unable to move! In the case of creating some order, though, depending upon who you are, you can expect a little pain.

When patterns are broken, new worlds emerge.
~ Tuli Kupferberg ~
Poet

For some people, managing tasks comes easy. They can't help it; it comes naturally. I know plenty of women who do not share that gift, and they constantly struggle to stay afloat. If you are in the latter category, be encouraged. Anything done over and over again will get easier with time. When it comes to managing events, remember:

Keep it simple.
Be consistent.
Customize your plans to work for you.

An important part of the IPPA system is to prioritize what needs to be done in your life. Don't forget to use the Opportunity Scale here and evaluate the cost. Be very sure that you are willing to pay the price before you commit to doing something.

The ABCs of Prioritization

My friend and business associate Jim Canfield has a way of prioritizing, using the ABCs:

- **A** items are "alligators" and will bite you in the butt if you don't give them attention now. These are truly urgent and very important issues. Delay at your own peril.

- **B** things are "bears" that are hibernating right now, but when they awake, they might eat you! These are important but not urgent. Be sure to address them when necessary, or they will ruin your day.

- **C** matters are "crows." They may be loud and obnoxious because they sound urgent, but they aren't very important. Don't fall prey to their call.

- **D** issues are plain "dogs." Oh, they may be cute, but they are not urgent or important. Be careful about spending time here, or your peace of mind may go to the dogs.

Whether you use the Priority Quadrant, the ABCs, or your own method, prioritize what matters most to you.

The "D" quadrant is probably where we lose the most time and receive the least back for it. These are trivial activities such as junk mail, email forwards, and idle chitchat that gobble up our time. Before know you it, you have wasted half your day. The internet has really become a time waster. Couple that with television, and we don't have enough hours in the day to get everything done. Well, we would have time if we managed these tasks a little better. Monitor them carefully. I had a client who got sucked into surfing the web five or six hours a day. She had to set an alarm in order to stop and get on to what really mattered. Granted, you may find these activities relaxing, but keep it in moderation—especially if you feel you just don't have enough hours in the day.

Lastly, items in the "C" quadrant can also tie us up. Examples are the telephone, a visitor, and other unexpected activities that are in your face but not necessarily important. By learning how to keep these brief, you can move on to what you need to do. I estimate that for every interruption you have while working on a project, you will need at least ten minutes to get refocused.

One of my clients decided to take the Priority Quadrant to heart, and he drew it on the big whiteboard in his office. Every morning, he would write out his tasks and assignments in the appropriate space. Over time, he had less and less in the crisis quadrant and more in the planning one. His stress went down and his productivity went up.

It Is T.I.M.E.

If you haven't reflected lately on what matters to you, I suggest you give it some consideration. You would think we all know exactly what we want, but we don't. I love the scene in the movie *Bruce Almighty* when Bruce, played by Jim Carey, gets in trouble because he gave all the people on his prayer list what they wanted. He wreaked havoc, and millions of people won the lottery! God, played by Morgan Freeman, asks Bruce, "Since when do people know what they want?" Thankfully, in real life God doesn't give us everything we ask for, but we should have some sense of what is important to us.

To help my clients decide what they want, I suggest that they look at it using the framework of T.I.M.E.

Tasks we need to accomplish

Interests we enjoy

Money matters

Energy

We are constantly balancing these four areas. Where are you spending most of your time? Do you focus mostly on work or career? Do you spend enough time with family, friends, and God? Are you stressing over money? Are you planning for your future, or carrying a lot of debt? Is your life energizing you, or are you being drained by it? The answers to these questions can be telling. If you feel one area is being slighted, start spending more time in it. Planning can help you do the other "stuff" more quickly, so you have the time available for what matters to you.

Planning Power

For every minute you spend planning, you will reap ten times the benefit! Planning provides clarity and concrete steps to ensure that the proper action will be taken. It can literally shorten the time it takes to get something done. What was it that you wanted to do with that extra thirty minutes? Planning will definitely give you more time to do it.

After you have identified and prioritized your tasks, be sure to add 20 percent to the time you think the tasks will take. And allow what I call "buffer spaces." When we pack our schedule so tightly that we do not have room for error, we've created a disaster waiting to happen. Murphy's Law tells us that what can go wrong, will go wrong! So, allow some space in between appointments. If you don't need it, fine. You can do some planning or maybe just enjoy the break.

Add 20 percent to your estimated time
and always have buffer spaces in your schedule

Personally, I plan using a combination of computer and hard copy. I am visual and like to see the month at a glance. When I leave the office, I can bring that or my tablet. Both have the same information. One client uses a three-ring binder. She hole-punches important papers and to-do lists and places them in the binder. This way, everything is in one place. It works for her. Figure out what works for you and use it.

Again, some folks rebel against getting this organized, saying it's not in their nature. Well, if you truly want more peace in your life, you will need to make some changes. Just remember that doing what you have been doing got you to a place you didn't like. If you want to be someplace else, you will need to do things differently.

ℭ

I love the story of the man who walks to work every day. One day he falls into a gigantic pothole. He never saw it coming. He has to climb out and is filthy as a result. He continues on his way. The next day, the man takes the exact same route and falls into the same pothole. He climbs out a little quicker this time but is still very dirty. The third day, he takes the same route but tries to step around the pothole. But alas, he still falls in and has to climb out. The fourth and fifth day, he takes the same route, trying to side step the pot hole, but he falls in, and climbs out. That night, he tells his wife about the pothole and how he keeps falling in. Her response: "Take a different route to work!"

Doing the same thing over and over again expecting different results IS insanity!

Chunk It Down

As you plan your tasks, don't try to take it on all one at once. This is a big mistake many people make. In fitness, it is the people who haven't exercised in five years. They go to the gym early in the morning and work out for four hours! After a few days, they are utterly exhausted and give up. They went too hard, too fast. Be cautious not to do the same thing with your projects, tasks, or events. If you have a major project to do at home, chunk it down into bite-size pieces.

How do you eat an elephant? One bite at a time!

Time-Out

No, I don't mean taking a time-out, although if you have been really bad and feel you deserve one, I'll wait! What I am referring to here is the practice of assigning due dates for projects. It's amazing how many people skip over this important step.

As you set due dates, be sure to allow enough time for each stage. I know I am constantly amazed at how long it takes to do relatively simple things, such making a doctor's appointment. I end up on hold for fifteen minutes. If I don't allow enough time to complete the task, then I fall behind. That is where "buffer time" comes in. As a way to help you consider all the steps, try the method I call RTP, to help you consider resources, time, and people.

RESOURCES	TIME	PEOPLE
What items will you need in order to do the project? Do you have them on hand, or will you have to buy them?	How much time will be required for each phase? Overestimate to allow for the unexpected delay.	Whose help will you need? Who is involved with the project? Who is responsible? Who is directly affected?

Be N.E.A.T.

To save time with paperwork, mail, and email, I've developed a method that I call N.E.A.T.

Needs action now – Urgent and important, so take care of it today.

Essential – Urgent but not important, so keep it handy.

Arrange it in a file – It is not urgent but may be important for future reference.

Toss it now not later – It is neither urgent nor important. Get rid of it.

Take Inventory

I have lived in California and Texas, both of which has extreme weather situations like earthquakes and hurricanes. My husband and I recently evaluated our evacuation plans, putting things in strategic places in case we needed to leave in a hurry, God forbid. As I went through the house, I started taking inventory of what we had and what I couldn't live without. This drill made me consider what was really important, and of course I realized I had been there before. During my divorce in 1997, I learned that all I really needed was my toothbrush, some clothes on my back, and my Bible. Everything else was just "stuff." Granted, I really enjoy the extras of life, but I realize I don't need as much as I sometimes think.

I pray you never have a tragic event or natural disaster, but I would encourage you to take inventory of your life. The more you have, the more work will be involved. For each item, ask some questions:

- Do you need it to survive?

- Do you need it for financial purposes?

- Is it required by law?

- Does it have extreme personal value to you?

- Is it irreplaceable?

A friend of mine realized he didn't like owning a home. He hated the work involved with it and felt trapped and tied down to it. Consequently, he bought a condo instead. He is much happier. Somewhere along the way, he had bought the house simply because it was the natural next step. Who says it has to be that way? Don't let society tell you what the American dream is—make your own! You will be much happier and less stressed.

> *Don't take anyone else's definition of success as your own.*
> *This is easier said than done!*
> ~ JACQUELINE BRISKIN ~
> *Writer*

Get Out of That Time Trap

Unlike my friend, I do enjoy owning a home. Gardening and cleaning the house are therapeutic to me. However, everyone is different, and because of that, we each have certain "time traps" that we can fall into and get stuck. A time trap is an event or attitude that can slow or even stop our productivity or forward momentum in achieving our goals. By recognizing, avoiding, or overcoming time traps, we can dramatically increase our success potential in all aspects of our life.

Two types of time traps exist: internal and external. Internal traps are those we impose upon ourselves, and the biggest of these is procrastination. Procrastination is probably the most common trap of all and is responsible for more disappointment, failure, and lost opportunities than all the other traps combined. Why, then, do we do it? People will often avoid something that they associate pain with. Unfortunately, not taking action will only make matters worse and increase the pain. Remember the Opportunity Scale? Using it is very helpful for folks who tend to procrastinate. Another effective technique is to do the hard stuff first and get it over with. Don't try to take too much on at once; chunk down your unpleasant task into manageable steps.

External traps are those that are imposed upon us. Some examples involve interruptions, waiting, and technology. Below are brief descriptions and some strategies to help you with these traps. When you can, take a different route!

TIME TRAP	DESCRIPTION	SOLUTION
Interruptions	Telephone, mail, visitors, meetings, and distractions	Set specific times to make phone calls. Let calls go to voicemail when possible. Keep your door shut. Ask visitors if they can come back or meet you later when it is more convenient. Make sure meetings are necessary, and stay on point!

Waiting	On people, on ideas, on materials, on input, or for direction.	Have agreed-upon deadlines and follow up ahead of time. Be proactive and get what you can as early as possible. Obtaining half of what you were promised is better than nothing. Document the deadlines and copy those involved so no miscommunication can occur.
Technology	Internet, email, cell phones, computers, voice mail, and the like were created to serve us; instead, we have become slaves to them.	Get back in the driver's seat! Use these devices as they were intended but don't allow them to control your life. Turn off the cell phone. Set times for internet and email. When you can, communicate in person.

Time management is much more than all of this and these traps. Look for another book by me soon to dive deeper into that! For now, be honest with yourself as to where you are getting sucked in and losing valuable energy and time. We've discussed a lot of principles. Use what works and also try some new things. By managing your time and events more effectively, you will truly see improvements in your life.

Moving Forward

The time is now for you to do this. You have reached a critical place, and you can't go backward. You must move forward if you wish to have a better future. I'm here to coach you, and don't forget to ask for God's help. I know that some of this can be overwhelming to you, so don't take it all on at once, and don't do it alone.

DEFY YOUR DIAGNOSIS CHAPTER THREE

FIT Life Formula @ Work

What is your #1 time trap?

Why do you think you fall into this repeatedly?

What one thing are you willing to do to combat it?

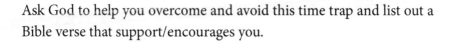

Ask God to help you overcome and avoid this time trap and list out a Bible verse that support/encourages you.

Who will be your accountability partner to keep you on track? Ask them within three days and set up weekly or biweekly touch basis via phone, email, text, social media, or in person.

CHAPTER FOUR

Stop Stressing!

Death is not the greatest loss in life.
The greatest loss is what dies inside of us while we live.
~ DR. NORMAN COUSINS ~
Journalist

The pace of life is moving along faster and faster. Almost everything can now be obtained through a drive-through window, including alcohol and prescription drugs. We are constantly bombarded by noise and media messages; even our cell phones get spam. The only time we slow down is when we sleep, but even then, some choose to "power sleep." Just reading that probably makes your heart race; I know typing it does for me! Here are some telltale signs that you are stressed to the max:

- You believe everyone around you has an attitude problem.
- You're using your cell phone to dial up every bumper sticker that says, "How's my driving? Call 1-800 …"
- Everyone's head looks like an invitation to batting practice.
- Everyone seems to have just landed here from outer space.
- You're sure that everyone is scheming to drive you crazy.

- The ibuprofen bottle is empty, and you bought it yesterday.

All this madness has to stop or we are going to drop dead—literally. We are seeing more and more illness, and I believe stress is the culprit. It's one of the reasons I mentioned stress so prominently in the introduction to this book. Whether we are struggling with time or event management or with emotional challenges, we *will* feel stressed. I wanted you to begin thinking about stress before we tackled it here; oftentimes we must understand our pain before we can prepare ourselves to fight it.

However, in this chapter I don't want to focus on the negative consequences of stress. You aren't where you want to be, and you know it. I want this chapter to be encouraging and inspiring for you. The last thing you need when feeling stress is more stress! So I am going to suggest a number of ways for you to manage your stress better. The suggestions may not be new to you, but my prayer is that I will be presenting them to you in a way that will make a positive impact. I believe you are ready for a change; otherwise, you wouldn't be reading this book.

> *Our dilemma is that we hate change and love it at the same time;*
> *what we want is for things to remain the same but get better.*
> ~ SYDNEY HARRIS ~
> *Journalist*

Again, try some things and see what works best for you. Personally, I love a hot bath. Typically, no problem is so big that I can't soak it away. My all-time favorite greeting card is one that says on the outside: *When I'm stressed, I take a nice, hot bubble bath.* The inside message reads: *I've been in here since last Thursday!*

Keep Your Sense of Humor

Our mothers were right: Laughter is the best medicine. Usually, though, our sense of humor is the first thing that goes when we are under pressure. In the classic movie *Mary Poppins*, one of my favorite scenes is when Uncle Albert, played by Ed Wynn, sings, "I love to laugh … loud and long and clear." You can't watch that part of the movie without starting to laugh yourself, because laughing is contagious. So laugh! Watch funny movies, read funny books, tell funny stories, and laugh at life. Laughing brings more oxygen to your body and gets your blood flowing. Try it. You can't be depressed *and* happy at the same time.

Smile

Did you know that it takes twice as many muscles to frown as it does to smile? I'm all for reducing wrinkles at the same time I lower my stress. How about you?

Try this: Stand up, slouch with your head down, and frown. Let your arms hang as if you can't move them. How do you feel? Probably low-energy and down—that's because your body is in a negative position. Now stand up nice and tall. Wave your arms around and jump for joy while you smile. Immediately you will have more energy and feel better. By putting your body in a more positive position, you are setting yourself up to feel better. Throughout the day, check yourself. If you are slouching, sit up straight.

CR

One evening driving home from work, I wondered why my rear-view mirror was always out of position at night. Who was moving it? I then realized, as I looked at myself in the mirror, that I was sunk down in the seat and hunched over like an old man. In the morning I sat up nice and tall. It wasn't the mirror that had moved; I wasn't in the same position at night because I slouched. Ironically, I would be exhausted when I arrived at home. So, I tried an experiment. I made a conscious effort to sit up straight on my car ride home at night, and you know what? I felt better ... and I could use my mirror without moving it.

Wake up with a smile and go after life.
Live it, enjoy it, taste it, smell it, feel it.
~ JOE KNAPP ~
Singer & songwriter

Have Fun!

What makes you smile? Sadly, the activities we enjoy the most are often the first things we stop doing when the stuff hits the fan or things get nuts. Try to weave back into your life something you love. Is it reading? Running? Knitting? Walking? Playing tennis? Visiting with friends? Whatever it is, make some time for it. Having fun will allow you to face the hard things in life with more enthusiasm. Visualize your energy as water in a cup. If you only pour it out, the cup will become empty rather quickly. You must do things to fill it back up. A little time spent on something you enjoy will give you extra energy to tackle difficult things.

Give a Little

In my own life, I realized how important it was for me to give to others when I was going through my divorce. I needed to focus on other people's problems, which made me realize how insignificant mine were by comparison.

Remember, God doesn't give us more than we can handle. You may be able to cope with something that would knock me to my knees, but I can deal with something that may be harder for you. All of us, though, benefit from giving back. A popular television commercial has a theme song, "Give a little love, and it all comes back to you." The ad features one man showing an act of kindness to a stranger. That stranger then does something for another stranger, and it gets passed along until the very end when the first man gets blessed. It came full circle.

"It is more blessed to give than receive."
~ ACTS 20:35 ~

Be Love

I really like the movie *Bruce Almighty*. When God (Morgan Freeman) is talking to Bruce (Jim Carey), he reminds Bruce that each of us should "be the miracle." We shouldn't sit there and wait on God to fix it for us; instead, we should try to fix it ourselves.

In the same way, we can "be love" to other people. We can be a light to the world and represent God. God works through you and me. If we are too stressed out to care for anyone else, then we are hindering God's plan. Do something for a neighbor. Bake them some cookies. Watch their dog. Call an elderly woman who is lonely and invite her to lunch. The world needs love; it needs you! And by giving, you will receive.

Know Your Limits

On the flip side of that is making sure you understand your own limits. For some of us, this is more difficult than for others. If you tend to give until it really hurts, you might benefit from the book *Growing Weary Doing Good?* by Karla Worley. Thinking only of others until you burn out isn't what God had in mind. Karla ended up in the hospital, and for months she couldn't be a wife, mother, sister, or friend. She learned that she had to set limits. The same is true for the rest of us. We have to know when enough is enough. What are your warning signs that you are totally spent? Do you get irritable? Are you short? Do you cry more frequently? Do you just want to sleep? Remember, you are just one person and can only do so much.

Protect Your Perimeter

The classic song "Don't Fence Me In," sung by Gene Autry, sums up Texas living. The best kinds of neighbors are those you don't see! I do like that catchy song, but it also reminds us that sometimes fences can be useful.

Think of your emotional energy as open land. If you have no fences, your energy flows without any restrictions. That may be exhilarating, but it also means that your door is wide open to anyone at any time. Fences serve a purpose. They keep in what we treasure and keep out what might threaten us. We can open the gate for friends and loved ones, but we also will be able to protect ourselves.

Maintain Margins

Think of the margins on a sheet of paper. They frame our words. Without them, people wouldn't be able to comprehend what we wrote. White spaces on paper—and in our lives—are what give us breathing room. Don't fill up every page so full that you can't breathe.

Christmas is a perfect example. It is a wonderful time of year, but many of us fill our schedules so completely that we lose the spirit of the holiday. Don't let this happen during the next Christmas season!

This year, cut back on your Christmas activities and go for quality. Do name draws for the family instead of giving gifts to every person, and make the gift more meaningful. Create a Christmas web page that people can visit rather than mailing a newsletter. Print up address labels instead of writing them out.

Simplify not only Christmas but also everyday events. During the dinner hour with your family, let the calls go to voice mail. That's what it's for! Suggest to friends and acquaintances that they call ahead of time before visiting so you can have the opportunity to say yes or no. Remember, the more in charge of your life you are, the less stress you will have from being out of control.

Set Boundaries

Have you ever said yes to something when you really wanted to say no? I think we all have. We need to say what we mean and mean what we say. Period.

**Say what you mean
and mean what you say.**

A book that has dramatically changed my life is *Boundaries*, by Drs. Henry Cloud and John Townsend. The premise is that we need to set boundaries in our relationships with family, friends, and co-workers. When do you say yes and when do you say no? It is different for each person, and every situation is different. We must be actively involved in the process in order to prevent getting stepped on or hurt.

When we say yes and we really wanted to say no, we aren't being authentic and true to ourselves. I know it's hard to say no, but we can soften the blow depending on how we say it. For example, if you are called by your child's teacher at eight o'clock in the evening and asked to bake twelve dozen cookies for the following day, you could say something like: "I could help out with a dozen or two." That doesn't sound like a no, but it is being realistic. If baking cookies is completely out of the question because of prior plans, then you might say something like this: "I would love to help next time if you could give me a little more notice." Wording can be the key to helping everyone feel okay.

Don't Forget to Say Yes

On the other end of the scale are some people who never say yes. In fact, we can all fall into this trap when stress is high. We say no to lunch with a friend, no to a massage that we desperately need, no to a nap—no to things that make us happy. Don't feel guilty about doing things for yourself!

Take Responsibility

Saying yes is really taking responsibility for ourselves instead of pointing the finger at others. If we are miserable, we really have no one to blame but ourselves. Don't get me wrong—I know people may have hurt you; I have been there. But we still have the choice as to how we will handle it. Being angry or withholding forgiveness hurts no one but us. It may feel good at the beginning, but it will eat you alive.

Acknowledge what you need and go after it. No one will think less of you or consider you selfish for caring for your own health. It is the responsible thing to do! Guess what happens when you are vibrant, healthy, strong, and positive? You have much more to give the world!

Be Authentic

Putting on an act doesn't help anyone. God made you who you are, so don't be ashamed of it; flaunt it! Besides, trying to be someone else takes a lot of energy. The more you try to cover up things or be a different person, the more energy you are losing. I don't know about you, but I need every bit of energy I can get my hands on.

Be true to yourself. That may mean you need to reflect on who you really are, what matters to you, and what you stand for, and that is okay. It's easy to lose yourself along the way, especially if you have had children. You've been a wife, a mother, a sister, a friend (back to all the hats we can wear). Who are you for *you*?

Know Your Mission

What is your purpose? Why are you here? If you haven't asked these questions yet, you need to. God has put each of us on this planet for a reason. It isn't necessarily what you are doing at work or even at home; it is the contribution to the world that only you can make, no matter what your role or what you are doing. I encourage you to write a personal mission statement that includes who you are in Christ, what your purpose is, and why you are here. Keep it somewhere handy. I have mine in my planner, and I review it often to remind myself that God has plans for me! When we are aligned with God and our mission, we become energized.

When you discover your mission, you will feel its demand. It will
fill you with enthusiasm and a burning desire to get to work on it.
~ W. Clement Stone ~
Businessman

Be All You Can Be!

You don't have to join the army to be your best. I believe that living out every day to the fullest is our gift back to God. He gives us life; what are we doing with it? Don't hold back. If you want to be silly, be silly. If you want to try something new for the sake of trying something new, go for it! We don't get any "do-overs" in life. Make the most of it and experience all you can.

Yoga Breathe

All the while, don't forget to breathe. When things are hectic and busy, we begin to take short, shallow breaths. This doesn't give us enough oxygen, and it results in fatigue. It creates a vicious cycle and can lead to sickness. Take time to breath deep every day.

Here's a great way to practice breathing that will take your stress level down immediately (don't try this while you are driving):

- Sit up nice and tall, shoulders back and head forward.

- Take a deep breath from all the way down in your lungs; lift your arms up to your sides while you do it until they are over your head and you have counted to ten.

- Hold your breath and keep your arms over your head for ten seconds.

- Slowly let your breath out as you lower your arms, counting to ten.

- Inhale and exhale normally.

- Repeat the process five times.

This exercise gives you a chance to get the stale air out and fill your lungs back up with fresh air. How did it make you feel? I can almost bet that you feel better and that your tension was reduced. If you try this in bed (you can omit the arms if you are lying down), you will probably fall asleep. This beats counting sheep every time!

Rest and Recharge

Resting is vital to stress management. Our brains work hard all day long. Sometimes the only time they actually get to rest is when we sleep. Even then, we can find it difficult to turn them off, can't we? Remember to breathe. Try a hot bath. A cup of chamomile tea works great for me right before bedtime. Whatever helps you to calm down and rest, do it before you hit the hay.

Research shows that those who sleep at least seven hours a night are thinner than those who sleep less than seven hours. When you don't get enough sleep, your body craves energy, and the way most people provide energy is through caffeine or sugar. The problem with these "quick fixes" is just that—they are fast to help but come crashing down just as fast. Good rest will provide your mind the strength it needs to function throughout the day without the junk.

We'll look at getting your health back in chapter 4, but for now, give your body some time to recharge. Our bodies, like our minds, can sometimes recover with a break. Stretching is an excellent way of helping the body after it has been taxed.

Renew

Don't forget your spirit through all of this. If your life has been out of control for a while, chances are that your spirit took a hit. Spend time with God—quiet, uninterrupted time just being with Him. Develop a heart of gratitude for all you have, and pray for those who are less fortunate.

Listen

Don't forget to listen. How easy it is to do all the talking. Then we wonder why God hasn't answered us. Well, he was waiting for us to shut up! Listen to his still, small voice. God oftentimes isn't in noise and activity but in a whisper.

> *"Then a great and powerful wind tore the mountains apart and shattered the rocks before the LORD, but the LORD was not in the wind. After the wind there was an earthquake, but the LORD was not in the earthquake. After the earthquake came a fire, but the LORD was not in the fire. And after the fire came a gentle whisper."*
> ~ 1 KINGS 19:11–12 ~

Circle of Influence

Lastly, I want to talk about your circle. Everyone has one. We have many things going on in our lives, and it's easy to worry and fret about them all. I want to suggest a better way to spend your energy.

Take a look at the circles below. The large circle represents your Circle of Concern. It includes *everything* you are concerned about: world peace, war, starvation in Africa, AIDS, Zika virus, killer bees, the drought, distant relatives—everything. These are things you're concerned about but have little control over. Maybe your job is more powerful than mine. Maybe you even have top-secret clearance. But still, you can only do so much. The things in our Circle of Concern are in God's hands, and we are called to pray *to* Him, not be Him.

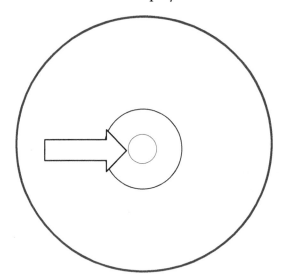

The second circle represents your Circle of Influence. These are things and people you can control or affect in some way, such as your family, neighborhood, community, and job. You can volunteer at the local shelter serving meals to homeless folks. You can vote and stay up to date on political issues. You can make sure your kids have all their shots. You can do something about your Circle of Influence, so why not spend more energy here? Spending energy worrying about what you cannot change is pointless. All you will get is tired, frustrated, stressed, and sick. Concentrate on what you can do.

Now let me ask you this: Can you make your family, friends, and co-workers do exactly what you want? No, but you can *influence* them. Because they respect, admire, and love you, they will consider it. But ultimately, the decision is theirs, isn't it? So do we really have control? Trying to control the world and the people in it will wear you out. Instead, try working on the only person you have complete control over: you.

The smallest circle is saved for us. It's called: My Attitude. Work on having a positive attitude no matter what, and you can be a change agent. Like smiles and laughter, positive attitudes are contagious.

> *Attitude is … the speaker of our present*
> *and the prophet of our future.*
> ~ JOHN C. MAXWELL ~
> *Bestselling author & pastor*

Kick the Stress Habit

Anything new will take a little getting used to, but I encourage you to get out of your stressed-out rut! You can get used to things being the way they are, even when you aren't happy about it. You deserve so much better, and I want you to have your life back. Start with something easy and build from there. But start. Okay?

> **I don't have Alzheimer's because**
> **I don't forget all the time. I must have**
> **"someheimers" though. Sometimes I remember**
> **and sometimes I don't!**

Get a Grip

Sometimes when things get bad, we must take a step back and evaluate what is going on. While we are in the thick of it, we can find it difficult to see the forest for the trees. Your first step, therefore, should be to S.T.O.P.

Stop

Think

Observe

Proceed

Whether you're in the middle of an argument with a spouse, a stressful debate at work, or trouble with your kids, *stop* long enough to assess the situation. Reacting without thinking can get us in trouble and create more stress, so *think* about what is happening. We have something between our ears called a brain; let's use it more often and think before we speak or act. We also have eyes, so *observe* how others are behaving and feeling. Any time we can put ourselves in their shoes, we will have more compassion and understanding. Then and only then, *proceed* and take your course of action.

Mistakes Happen

Alas, we are human, and occasionally we will stick our foot in our mouth or do the wrong thing. Instead of beating yourself up over it, learn from it. I think women are much harder on themselves then men, who seem to be able to file it away and move on. For many of my women friends, too much energy is wasted on the "shoulda, coulda, woulda's" of life. Change gears and start putting energy into learning from your mistakes so you can do it better the next time.

How does God teach us to be patient? By giving us situations that try our patience! Trust me; God will present another opportunity for you. Practice makes perfect—or at least better.

Extend G.R.A.C.E.

Ever see the commercial that says, "We don't live near perfect. That's why there is Walgreens"? Not one of us here on earth is perfect. The only perfect man was nailed to a tree. To expect others and ourselves to be perfect is unrealistic. Your children will make mistakes. Your friends will let you down. Your husband will hurt you by doing or saying the wrong thing. Don't put pressure on those you love to be perfect. Instead, give them some grace and understanding.

We must allow people to be who they are and to do the best that they can, which is all any of us can do. It doesn't mean you should let people deliberately injure you or slack off from responsibilities, but it does mean you should weigh what is truly important.

Ladies, I think that sometimes we are awful about expecting things our way, especially in the house. If your husband vacuums but doesn't do as good a job as you would, concentrate on his gift and not on how he did. If your son or daughter puts the dishes away but in the wrong place, thank them, don't scold them. Extend G.R.A.C.E.

Give **R**espect.

Appreciate and **C**ompliment **E**fforts.

As [a man] thinketh in his heart, so is he.
~ PROVERBS 23:7, KING JAMES VERSION ~

Think Positively

Thinking positively has power. I play tennis, and for the longest time I would yell at myself in my head when I made mistakes. I would call myself names like "stupid" or "idiot" every time my shot didn't go where I wanted it to. My game would go from bad to worse, and I would get so frustrated that I didn't want to play anymore. Then I read *The Inner Game of Tennis*, by W. Timothy Gallwey. His book doesn't tell you how to play tennis but what to think. He has similar books on just about every sport. What he teaches is to not attack yourself when you make a mistake but instead to address the mistake.

For instance, when I hit the ball too low, I need to correct my swing to make the ball clear the net. Or if I hit the ball too long and it goes out of the court, I need to adjust my power a bit to keep it in. Focus on what you need to do differently rather than tearing yourself apart. The world will make plenty of attempts to drag you down; you don't need to join in.

If you find yourself repeating the same mistake over and over again, look at it objectively. What are you doing wrong? What could you do differently? Getting on your own case won't help you overcome the mistake. In fact, it will probably ensure that you remain stuck. But thinking positively can help you move on.

Look Forward, Not Back

Speaking of the future, don't look back. Yes, we need to know our past mistakes so that we can learn from them, but don't get stuck there. We all make mistakes. Name them, acknowledge them, and move on. Too often, we spend our energies worrying about what we may not be able to become, instead of becoming it.

Ever find yourself saying, *I do not want to become my mother?* Or, *I don't want a marriage like my in-laws?* Don't concentrate on what you lack or don't want to become; instead, focus your energies on developing yourself and adding those things to your life that you want. By focusing on the negative, we are only looking at what isn't working or what we don't like. We have to put on new glasses and begin looking for the things we do like and want.

Know What You Want

We must first know what we want—what we *really* want. What matters to you the most? What kind of life do you want? When you embarked on getting your life back, what did you have in mind? I'm not talking about general statements like peace, love, and joy. Of course, we want those, but what do they look like in real life? The more specific we get, the clearer the picture in our minds of what we are aiming for.

We'll never hit the target if we don't know what it looks like, so let's take a moment and have you check the words that signify what you want rather than looking at where you are right now. Check all that apply (they are in no special order):

- Healthy conflict
- Civil disagreements
- Respect of differing opinions
- Acceptance of who I am today
- Encouragement to grow
- Honest prayer
- Heartfelt gratitude
- Appreciation
- Support
- Thoughtfulness
- Kindness
- Partnership
- Shared responsibility of household chores
- Engaged conversations
- Intimacy

- Closeness

- Other_____

The list could go on and on, but at least this is a start. Visualize the kind of life and marriage you want and keep these in the forefront of your mind. Toss out the negative images and replace them with your future life!

You Matter

Men in particular seem to struggle with their identity outside of what they do. Their job or career is who they are, and when they retire, they often don't know what to do. Statistically, a high percentage of men die within their first year of retirement. I fear that we are getting caught up in this same identity issue. We are wives, mothers, sisters, friends, executives, and volunteers—an array of hats. We give to others in all sorts of ways, and we can get suckered into believing that who we are is defined by what we do. But it is not. Who we are is much bigger than that and God wants us, not our accomplishments.

In 1997, when I almost couldn't move because my weight had dropped to 97 pounds, I almost lost hope. God provided a vision to me. I've never had that happen before or since; it was like watching a movie but without sound, and I was in it.

I saw myself walking down a dirt road. I was extremely tired from the divorce; I was hungry; I was overwhelmed with grief over my mom's death; and I was lugging all my belongings in one massive black suitcase on wheels. I could barely move it, and I was crying uncontrollably. I would take a few steps and then would drop the suitcase because it was just too heavy. I sobbed harder and fell to the ground. As I wailed in anguish, I exclaimed, "I can't go on! I can't do this anymore." My head fell into my hands.

Moments later, I saw two dusty feet in canvas sandals through my hands. As I looked at them, I could tell they had walked a lot of miles. I lifted my head slowly and saw a worn-out robe tied with a rope. Suddenly, I found myself looking into the eyes of Jesus. His eyes soothed me immediately. Without a word, He pulled me up off the ground and wrapped His arms around me. As He held me closer, my weeping grew deeper—straight from my soul.

All the things I had done and not done rushed through me. A list of things I was supposed to do hit me like bricks. Jesus began walking me down the road, but I stopped. I forgot my bag, which was still on the ground behind us. I turned to reach for my stuff, but He shook His head no. He drew me close … right to His heart. And from His heart I heard this: *You are what matters to me, not your material possessions or what you do.* The message poured from His heart into mine, and we began walking again. I left the suitcase behind, and my tears subsided.

I began to regain strength. At eight o'clock that night, I got out of bed (I had been physically unable to before) and began a life of handling my stress better. I've never been the same since.

God loves *you.* Knowing that you don't have to perform for Him should dramatically reduce your stress. We put pressure on ourselves, but instead we need to love ourselves as He loves us.

Love is the highest, purest most precious of all spiritual things.
It will draw out from men their magnificent potential.
~ ZIG ZIGLAR ~
Motivational speaker

DEFY YOUR DIAGNOSIS CHAPTER FOUR

FIT Life Formula @ Work

What are you doing that contributes to your stress? Are you a workaholic, egotistical, materialistic, or control freak?

Are you sabotaging your own life by being passive-aggressive or running away from things instead of confronting them?

What do you want your new, balanced life to look like? The more specific you are, the better the chances you'll create it.

What needs to go (eliminated or delegated) in order to free up space for what really matters to you?

What's your top priority in order to move toward less chaos and more balance?

CHAPTER FIVE

Change From the Inside Out

Love yourself. It is important to stay positive
because beauty comes from the inside out.
~ JENN PROSKE ~
Actress

Women have struggled with their appearances since the beginning of time when Eve hid from God in the garden. With increased media messages and outlets telling women how they should look, talk, and walk a certain way, women's confidence and self-esteem has been plummeting. Weight loss products are a billon (yes, that's with a b) dollar industry because women have been sold the belief their outward appearance is all that matters and their happiness and success depend upon their looks. What rubbish!

As a result of that garbage, we are left longing for whatever "it" is we believe we do not have, and desperately seeking acceptance from the world around us. We think we can never be pretty enough or thin enough. And the kicker? Because of our low self-esteem, we settle and align ourselves with real losers, thinking we are the ones who aren't good enough. ENOUGH is right! We must stop living in fear and break free from this bondage so we can create a better life for ourselves. If you do not believe you deserve better, believe me when I say YOU DO! We must redirect our focus and change ourselves from the inside out.

How Did I Get Here?

As far back as I can remember, I was never satisfied with my body. I wanted to be taller, thinner, and prettier. I *always* felt fat. Besides having a 300-plus-pound sister, my mother's obsessive control and need for perfection profoundly impacted me. I became consumed with "measuring up." My dad also died when I was the tender age of thirteen, and research has proven time and time again how a young girl's image of herself is formed by the way her father treats her. What a huge loss. Although in reality I was already tall, thin, and attractive, I was trapped in a large-sized and ugly image of myself. What I saw in the mirror was not reality. Unfortunately, I know I am not alone.

Women are subjected daily to the world's view, and in particular Hollywood's, of how they should look and live. If you ever doubt Hollywood's power, just take a stroll down memory lane: Marilyn Monroe to Twiggy and back again. Whatever the top actresses and models look like is the new bar to clear. Add to the mix cosmetic surgery and Photoshop perfection of images so celebrities look like plastic dolls, and no normal person can ever clear the bar. By the way, I'm not against plastic surgery all together. What I do oppose is the obsession with it resulting from insecurities. Our response to people like Michael Jackson and Elizabeth Taylor should have been one of grave concern and sympathy. Instead, however, we attempt to meet unrealistic expectations of perfection. Some restrict calories to the point of anorexia while others eat themselves sick, suppressing their feelings of inadequacy with food, alcohol, or drugs. These unhealthy responses create a vicious cycle; we feel worse and do more of whatever isn't healthy. The reality is our mirror is warped, deceiving, and lying to us, ladies. The problem is we keep looking for our significance in the *wrong* place. We need new mirrors!

Curve:
The loveliest distance between two points.
~ MAE WEST ~
Actress

A cartoon I love to this day is too close to the truth to make me laugh. It is one of a bald, fat, and gross man staring into a mirror. The reflection he sees is of a masculine stud, muscles bulging with a six-pack. In other words, he thinks quite highly of himself despite the truth he is obese. The next frame is a gorgeous, fit, and trim woman with curves all in the right places who sees an overweight, disgusting, and ugly monster looking back at her from the mirror. She cannot see reality. Unfortunately, the cartoon is spot-on. Research has proven men tend to date about two to three levels *above* their "class" while women date two to three levels *beneath* them. Men also seem to have the ability to look at other men and say, "Wow, he has great abs!" or,

The Difference Between Women & Men

"He's got killer biceps" without feeling insecure. They typically do not get wrapped up in comparing themselves to others. Women, on the other hand, rip apart, piece by piece, every woman they see and compare every square inch of their body to others. They feel either jealous or inferior. How exhausting and futile! Men must have better mirrors.

Defective Mirrors

In all seriousness, our mirrors did get damaged somewhere along the line. Our reflections became distorted and our self-image deranged. As I mentioned, my challenge with my appearance goes way back. Heck, I can remember looking at my Barbie doll's perfect figure and wondering what went wrong with me. Why did my chest look more like Ken's? Things only got worse when every other girl in junior high and high school developed breasts, and I was *still* waiting. If we are to stand a chance of seeing ourselves differently, then we will need to BREAK the old mirror, shattering it into a million pieces.

Accepting ourselves for who we are and what we look like starts with seeing ourselves through the eyes of God instead of from our earthly mirrors. Okay, this is easy to say but is *very* difficult to do, especially if you attended church and were told how unworthy you were. Women spend hundreds of dollars on makeup and clothes, and thousands of dollars on fitness and weight loss products each year. Unfortunately, we never feel better. Actresses and models can't even keep up anymore. They just get more nips, tucks, lifts, and liposuction. Add insult to injury with airbrushed, computer-enhanced images provided by Hollywood, and we are left feeling completely inadequate, to say the least. We are all in trouble when even Julia Roberts isn't good enough for her own role in *Pretty Woman*. Those are not her legs!

I think the time has come to acknowledge we are in a race that is impossible to win. Once and for all, we must admit we are not perfect. The older I get, I am relieved at this truth. The pressure is off. I no longer feel the need to participate in a crazy, unwinnable race. As Popeye says, "I am what I am!" Thankfully, we are all made different. How boring the world would be if we really did look alike.

Celebrate your uniqueness. If you struggle each and every time you look in the mirror, then get rid of the stupid thing … or break it! That's what I did. I couldn't be trusted around them, so I broke mine into a million pieces. The exercise was quite liberating. Until you can appreciate how God made you, you may need to stay clear of mirrors, as well.

Good Enough for Today

And the way we start improving our self-image is accepting we are good enough for today. We may actually need to lose a little weight, show some signs of aging with wrinkles, and might need a new hairdo, but for today, we are *good enough*. In her book *Simple Abundance,* Sarah Ban Breathnach encourages us to thank our body parts for what they do. Rather than fight with them, accept them. Start with those aspects of your body you already like and move on to the ones you wish were different. Focus on what those body parts *do* for you. I have always loved my eyes as they change color depending upon what I wear, but I have forever despised my thunder thighs. Through the years as I have applied Sarah's suggestion, I have learned to appreciate those strong legs of mine. They carry me up mountains, allow me to snow shoe, run, and play tennis—all things I love to do. By switching my attitude, I spit in the face of the world's unrealistic view and became free!

Most of us can easily list out our many faults, but when asked to write out our attributes, we get stuck. Recruit the help of a trusted, dear friend to draft up your list of positives. Then, work on being grateful for the good, and accepting and appreciating other features. Choose to love yourself, because you are indeed good enough!

Life Isn't Perfect

I think we also need to acknowledge life isn't perfect. Walgreens says it right in their commercials, "Since we don't live in perfect, we have Walgreens instead." Life is what happens every day when we are waiting for something amazing to happen. The reality is, day in and day out, we go about a normal life. We have, and will, make mistakes, which has consequences. Hopefully, we will learn from the choices we made when we were younger and make better ones as we love ourselves more.

People will hurt, disappoint, and even betray us. Even as we grow stronger in our self- acceptance, we cannot control others. We cannot make someone else let go of their anger or hate and decide to love themselves and others. What we can do, however, is align ourselves with other like-minded people. I cannot stress how important this is; we must choose our friends wisely. We must be even pickier with those whom we give our heart. I swear, women spend more time considering their bank than they do the men they date. In other words, we value and treasure our money more than ourselves. Thankfully, the pressure to marry isn't as great today as it once was, allowing women the time to reflect and decide if they really want to marry. I'm pleased to see more single women choosing careers and adventures over settling down. I'm married, so please do not misunderstand my message. I'm not against good relationships, but the philosophy of "a bad relationship is better than no relationship at all" cannot continue. We must all let go of old ways, bad habits, and self-destructive behaviors.

Hurt people hurt people.
~ WILL BOWEN ~
Author

Release the Old You

I love the word *release*. I picture opening my hands and letting a bird fly away to its freedom. Contrary is the word lose. People want to lose weight, but what usually happens? Their extra weight finds them again! Well, of course it would; it was lost and now it is found. Stinking thinking and bad habits need to be released. We don't need them anymore. They haven't served us well; in fact, they have *harmed* us.

If, like me, you have kept a journal, you may have some toxic thoughts and feelings on those pages. The process is healing as we let go of what is inside of us and place it in the journal. However, those dark, nasty, and often negative words still have life on those pages. I encourage you to go through the exercise of burning your journal. Find a gal pal to partner up with. You can locate a fire pit on the beach, like I did once, and as the pages burn up in flames, dance around the pit. They are released and no longer your responsibility. My friend and I then ran into the ocean to signify the start of new patterns and more positive thoughts. Others have hiked deep into the woods and buried their journals, one torn and shredded piece at a time. As they ripped more pages, their anger subsided and was released. They were free to feel good again. As simple as this sound, the process can be quite powerful.

If that doesn't suit you, find something that does. Counselors can be a great sounding board, as long as you have a specific goal in mind. Set a time limit to address your concern, and then take action. A new you is awaiting!

Let Go

I used to hate my old self. I would beat it up on a regular basis with comments such as, *How could you be so stupid? What were you thinking, really? You're a complete idiot!* I would vacillate between feelings of embarrassment and disappointment. Embarrassed in the sense of what others might think of me because of my mistakes and disappointment in myself that I should have known better. Again, I know I am not alone. Many women struggle with guilt, low self-esteem, anger, and a myriad of other emotions. Here is the secret: Those emotions only have power over you when *you* let them. When we hold on to those negative thoughts and feelings, we build our own prison. In turn, only we have the power to unlock the gate and walk free.

Some of us think holding on makes us strong,
but sometimes it is letting go.
~ Herman Hesse ~
Poet

DEFY YOUR DIAGNOSIS CHAPTER FIVE

FIT Life Formula @ Work

Thinking back over your life, what would you say have been the most difficult times of your life?

What life hurts have been difficult for you to shake?

Have the traumas and painful events altered your self-image?

List at least ten positive things about yourself:

Write a letter from God to yourself sharing how HE sees you.

CHAPTER SIX

Be Brave! Courage Comes From Suffering

Courage is the commitment to act, even if you are afraid.
~ MARK SANBORN ~
Motivational speaker & bestselling author

In 1999, I began having strange symptoms. I had horrible joint pain and swelling. After about nine months, I could barely hold a glass of water. I was struggling with fatigue, muscle weakness, and a chronic cough. Little did I know I was embarking on a long and frustrating journey to not only find out what I had, but curing it. In March 2006, I was finally diagnosed with Lyme disease.

I didn't know much about Lyme disease, as it wasn't given much attention in the health community back when I fought it. Thankfully, more attention is being given to this horrific disease, but I quickly discovered most doctors have only a basic understanding of the disease and are not really equipped (unless they do additional research on their own) to diagnose or treat the disease. In a nutshell, a bacterium called *Borrelia burgdorferi* found in mice, squirrels, and other small animals gets transmitted through ticks to humans when they bite. This bacterium then lives in the human body, often hiding in our cells, and they work hard to make the environment (our body) comfortable for them, which can mean lowering our body temperature. When they do die, they release a toxin, and humans get sick. Symptoms vary person to person. Mine looked a lot like rheumatoid arthritis, yet I didn't have the markers; I just had the swelling and pain.

Originally, experts thought Lyme disease could only be transmitted through deer ticks in certain areas; however, some health professionals are now seeing it through fleas and blood transfusions. The real bummer is many folks will never truly be correctly diagnosed; therefore, they will never get better. People who are not properly diagnosed will be treated for rheumatoid arthritis, MS, or a slew of other false diagnoses leading to more pain and suffering. Lyme's is indeed the great imitator! I'm grateful I was introduced to a man who specializes in Lyme disease, and he joined me in the quest to beat it and reclaim my health. I literally had to go to war.

The Battle for My Life

Every year since my first episode, I would have a horrendous outbreak of pain and swelling. It would jump from joint to joint. Primarily, it would affect my fingers and wrists, but it started hitting my shoulders and feet. Nothing would help. And trust me, I tried everything: chiropractic care, acupuncture, energy balancing, massage, heat therapy, cold treatments, natural herbs, cleanses, juice fasts, exercise, rest, etc. If man knows it, I tried it!

Then, in December of 2005, I began to have another outbreak. Each year, the pain got more intense, and the episodes would last longer. Instead of weeks, my outbreaks would last for months. I also began to have mental fog, which was the last straw for me. I was beyond discouraged. And at my lowest point, my ex-husband began harassing me again with statements such as, "Glad to see God is punishing you for divorcing me. You deserve to suffer!" Wow, really? This only made me more determined to beat this disease and come through the other side!

Doctors would look at the individual problems but not the whole. No one was able to connect the dots. I was told time and time again, "You are healthy, and nothing is wrong with you." I finally took matters into my own hands and began researching on the internet. Lyme's matched my symptoms most closely, and I had been on a hike seven years prior up on the tick-infested Central Coast of California, where we lived for four years. I took an online quiz with the Canadian Lyme Disease Foundation and matched many of the symptoms (www.can-lyme.com). I took this to my local doctor and said, "I think I should have tests run." She agreed. She warned me, as did everything I read, how Lyme's can test negatively even if you have it. Lyme disease is very difficult to detect because it affects a number of systems, such as brain, central nervous, autonomic nervous system, cardiovascular, digestive, respiratory, muscular-skeletal, etc. But I wanted to get to the bottom of this once and for all!

Mixed Emotions

My first antibody blood test was negative. As I shared my situation with my chiropractor one day, he informed me how he just heard a man speak on the subject. He provided me with his number, and I called Dr. Steven C. Davis in Palo Cedro, CA (www.drddc.com). Dr. Davis has cured over 75,000 people of Lyme disease in his career. He also has a specific test for Lyme called the QRiBb, so I took it. It wasn't cheap, about $250, but at that point, I didn't care. I needed help! The pain was growing and spreading. Moving, walking, and exercising hurt, and I wasn't sleeping. My results showed I was off the chart with pathogens (bugs), and the blood work confirmed I had *Borrelia burgdorferi* in my system. I had Lyme disease.

After six long years, I finally knew why I felt so bad. I had an array of emotions: anger, relief, frustration, disappointment, and fear. Now what? I wondered. Treating Lyme's is just as difficult as discovering you have it. Shortly after my diagnosis, a professional football player died from complications with Lyme disease. Old school thoughts are that it can't be cured, but please, if you get anything out of this, know recent research shows it *can* be cured—it just takes time.

Suffering in Silence

Living with something that can't be seen or touched has its pros and cons. The good news is, no one has to know you have it. The bad news is, no one will know you have it unless you tell him or her, which equates to very little support. Even when I have shared with people my news, they would go, "Oh, that's too bad." Friends and family never really comprehended the pain and suffering I dealt with day in and day out. No one called to check in and see how I was doing; no one sent cards or flowers. Their lives went on. Yet Lyme's can be dangerous and life-threatening if untreated. In fact, the process of killing off the bacteria can put you in the hospital, and even when you do beat it, you may have consequences that linger. Today, they are comparing Lyme disease to cancer. It is as difficult to diagnosis and just has tough to bet. And when you do, you will never be the same. I have forever been changed by it and live with its parting gifts.

I'm a fighter (inherited trait from my mother) and have kept pressing on despite how I have felt. I am also a fitness professional and a very active individual. I've had days when I could barely get out of bed, but I went to work anyway, which required more physical ability than I had. Pressing on took incredible amounts of energy to focus beyond my ailment. I've often felt like crawling into a black hole and giving up, but I didn't and haven't. For anyone experiencing a dark time—whether emotional, physical, mental, or spiritual—I pray you hang in there. We must beat our adversary and live on in victory!

Pain with a Purpose

My ordeal has spanned over 19 years and counting. I have beaten the disease but continue to live with residual effects. Some days are better than others. God has allowed me to use my experience to encourage, support, and love others through their journeys. I try to remind people our pain really does have a purpose. God created pain so we might pay attention. Touch fire, and you get burned. You know immediately. Ouch! Other pain requires us to ease up or back off of exercise, like a sprained ankle or pulled muscle. Pain is a good thing, but I can attest that when we have chronic pain, it certainly does not feel that way. At these times, we must trust and believe God's promises. He isn't striking us down and punishing us, like some hurtful, sick people may suggest. He is walking along side of us *through* our journey. He will provide what we need, and He will give us strength.

While I was living in Texas, my acupuncturist was actually from China, and he framed pain in a new way for me. He said, "In my country, those who live the longest are those whose bodies fight the hardest." I had not thought of my hyper immune system that way. I was focusing on the downside: chronic inflammation. However, he was right. Like anything, how do we know what to do if we don't have any practice?

Webster's dictionary actually describes pain as "localized physical suffering associated with bodily disorder (as a disease or an injury)." To those who deal with pain day in and day out, more appropriate terms could be misery, unhappiness, depression, despair, and hopelessness. But pain at the very basic level is our body's signal that something is wrong. Without it, we wouldn't know a stove was hot and could burn our skin off. All pain is not bad. In fact, certain pain can prevent us from serious injury.

When we are no longer able to change a situation,
we are challenged to change ourselves.
~ *Victor Frankl* ~
PSYCHIATRIST

Our attitude makes all the difference. Most of us are familiar with the cycle of grief: shock, denial, anger, bargaining, depression, testing, and then acceptance. Those with chronic pain need to understand how much grieving is associated with their illness: loss of good health, physical abilities, and future possibilities. Unlike events and situations with a beginning and an end, chronic pain continues, often paralyzing us and preventing us from completing the cycle.

Asking, *Why me?* is a natural part of the process; however, we can drive ourselves insane trying to find answers. If you haven't gotten angry, you will. The bottom line: bad things happen to good people. The challenge for us is to not get stuck in the M.U.D.: madness, unhappiness, and depression.

Anger is like mud. Once we step in it, it gets a hold on us, and we have difficulty getting out. Express your anger: throw rocks, scream, cry, talk to a friend, journal—let it out. Then, choose to not live there. Put your energy to good use—like fighting your battle!

I encourage people to make the shift from being angry about their situation to being angry at their ailment. This can make the difference between being a victim to victor; from passively surviving to conquering your fears and disappointments.

I know God will not give me anything I can't handle.
I just wish that He didn't trust me so much.
~ MOTHER TERESA ~
Saint

Anger can serve us well, as long as we aren't mad at God or our circumstances. Instead, we can turn our anger at the illness and commit to destroying it to the best of our ability. We must also be willing to accept what help God gives us. We may focus so much on complete and total healing that we forget the blessings along the way. Keep your eyes peeled, because they show up … and in the strangest places.

Although we may not know our exact purpose of our suffering, our faith allows us to know God has a plan. For me, I have learned the valuable lesson of letting others love me. I am a very independent sort, and asking for help has never been easy for me. To this day, I still don't run around sharing on Facebook how bad I feel. I choose to concentrate on the good things. However, a select few know the true story. These are friends who pray for me and offer to help. They are a treasure! In order for them to give, though, they must know how I am *really* doing. I also realized being a super woman was highly overrated. No one was demanding I be one; I put the Wonder Woman suit on myself. I am able to say no to things I would have taken on before simply for the challenge. I have nothing to prove to anyone, including myself. I have fought a bloody battle, and I have won!

> *Pain nourishes courage. You can't be brave if you've*
> *only had wonderful things happen to you.*
> ~ MARY TYLER MOORE ~
> *Actress*

Be Brave!

I don't know exactly what you might be facing, but I can say with confidence you are not alone. You may feel very much alone at times, but you must lean upon God, His strength, and His love. Let Him carry you if you must, but do not give in to the lies of the enemy. We gain insight and wisdom during our difficult times, much more so than when things are going hunky-dory. I don't know who wrote this, but I've kept it for years now:

> *To realize the value of a sister, ask someone who doesn't have one.*
> *To realize the value of ten years, ask a newly divorced couple.*
> *To realize the value of four years, ask a graduate.*
> *To realize the value of one year,*
> *ask a student who has failed a final exam.*
> *To realize the value of one month,*
> *ask a mother who has given birth prematurely.*
> *To realize the value of one week, ask an editor of a newspaper.*
> *To realize the value of a day, ask someone who works outdoors.*
> *To realize the value of just one hour,*
> *ask the lovers who are waiting to meet.*
> *To realize the value of a single minute,*
> *ask a person who has missed the train.*
> *To realize the value of one second,*
> *ask a person who has survived an accident.*
> *To realize the value of one millisecond,*
> *ask the person who won an Olympic silver medal.*
> *Time waits for no one. Treasure every moment you have. You will trea-*
> *sure it even more when you can share it with someone special.*
> *To realize the value of a friend, lose one.*
> ~ ANONYMOUS ~

I would add to this list our health. We don't know how good we have it until we don't. I always strived for a healthy life, but I now appreciate my abilities. I don't whine (well, not as often) about wrinkles, aging vision, and other factors associated with growing older. I'm thankful to be alive! Ask anyone who has almost lost their life to a disease or tragedy, and you will hear a renewed sense of gratefulness. Regardless of your viewpoint of Lance Armstrong, he fought cancer and won. Nothing else scared him. He had such courage to face anything else life threw at him, and the same is for us all. We are warriors, taking on the battles presented to us, one at a time. We may need to put our sword down and rest a bit, but we keep fighting. We press on, and we move forward. Why? This is *our* life, a gift to be experienced and lived to the fullest. Don't settle for anything less. Go, fight, and win!

You will never do anything in this world without courage.
It is the greatest quality of the mind next to honor.
~ ARISTOTLE ~
Philosopher

DEFY YOUR DIAGNOSIS CHAPTER SIX

FIT Life Formula @ Work

Have you struggled with health issues that were dismissed or misdiagnosed? How did this make you feel?

During your trials, did you share your fears with anyone? Did they support you or hurt you?

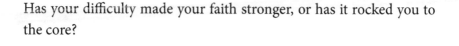

Has your difficulty made your faith stronger, or has it rocked you to the core?

Are you angry? At God? At yourself? Spouse? Family? Friends? Write and list it all out on paper and then burn it (in safe conditions). As the flames rise up to the heavens, turn all your anger over to God.

CHAPTER SEVEN

Let Go and Let God

Let go of yesterday. Let today be a new beginning and be the best that
you can, and you'll get to where God wants you to be.
~ JOEL OSTEEN ~
Pastor & bestselling author

I just recently watched *Conversations with God*, based upon the book by Neale Donald Walsh, which I have read a couple of times. This true story is about how a man's life went to pieces very quickly. When he hit rock bottom and was in the heights of his pity party, God reached out to him and asked one question: *Have you had enough?* This was quite the question for a man who once was a radio show host and was now homeless, eating out of garbage cans. Neale wasn't sure how to take the question, and I suspect we would be confused as well. Regardless if we subscribe to Neale's religion or not, the profound enlightenment his story offers is like sunshine on a cloudy day. How refreshing to think God is waiting upon us to accept all the good He has for us. All we need to do is just believe things can and *will* be better.

Have you had enough? Are you done with drama? Are you tired of beating yourself up and reliving mistakes time and time again? Are you ready to leave the old you behind and create someone happier? Until we are ready, we will not receive it … ever. Only you know when you have hit your rock bottom. We are all on different time tables, thus I cannot judge anyone else for their choices. We do the best we can for the time, but our life can be better!

Letting Go

I can recall a time in my life when I was hunched over on the floor because I didn't have the strength to sit up or stand. I was bawling my eyes out in despair. I felt utterly broken after my divorce. I held a management position, I was responsible for a staff of five people and a hefty budget, yet I couldn't seem to get my own life together. Through the tears, I saw a vision of scattered puzzle pieces on the floor. They were everywhere with no rhyme or reason. A mixture of colors and sizes, they didn't appear to all go together. I cried harder. "Great, now I can't even figure out where these stupid puzzle pieces go!"

God spoke quietly to my heart. *You don't need all these pieces, dear one. Some of them just aren't you. Let them go.*

His words took a few moments to sink in. *You mean, I don't have to pick up ALL these pieces of my broken life?*

Again, God tenderly reached out to my heart. *Only the ones that suit and serve you.*

After some time passed and I gained my composure, I went through a visualization of vacuuming up all the mismatched, ugly, wrong, and unwanted pieces. I was left with fewer pieces to compile. I had a renewed sense of hope. Perhaps putting my life back together wouldn't be impossible!

A Shift

I have always wished the best for my friends, praying fervently for their success and happiness. In relationships, I gave my all to helping *their* dreams come true. Once again, men have an advantage over women, as they are singularly focused on what *they* want and need. I'm not bashing men here but appreciating an aspect of their wiring that is different than women's. Women can become so others focused we forget about our own needs. We should learn from men yet again by remembering what we see out in the world—what we desire—*can* be ours. We can create new patterns, behave differently, think more positively, and make a new life for ourselves.

For me, breaking down allowed me to rebuild a new me, which was stronger and more confident in whom I was *becoming*. Who I was back then is NOT who I am today, and with God's grace, I hope the person I am tomorrow is even better than who I am right now! I find incredible hope in the truth we are not our past, nor do we have to become what and how we were raised. We do not have to be like our mothers, nor do we have to lower ourselves to some men's, and much of the world's, view of us. We are in the driver's seat of our own life! God is our co-pilot, offering directional assistance when we are confused or unclear as to which way to turn. But we must grab the wheel with both hands, put our foot on the gas, put the car in gear, and drive forward!

Listen Carefully

One of the challenges of deciding on a new direction is that old patterns don't die easily. In fact, their voices linger in our heads for quite some time, vacillating from quiet whispers to loud screams. I have found we have four voices in our head: God's, our soul's, our spirit's, and Satan's. Let me first distinguish between our soul and our spirit. Arthur Burke of Plumbline Ministries has done an incredible job of bringing clarity to something that was foggy for me most of my life. Our spirit is our connection to God. Our spirit is hope, love, joy, and peace—everything good. Our spirit is heaven bound and sees only potential. Our soul, on the other hand, is where all our experiences here on earth reside. That means all our hurts and wounds are the souls only reference. This is where fear lives in us. Even when our spirit is growing in faith and trust, our soul's voice is the one who pooh-poohs it, discounts it, and says we'll only get burned if we try something new.

I struggled with this concept at first. We're taught the soul is what leaves us and joins God when we die, but it is actually our spirit reconnecting with its Maker. Our soul certainly makes us "us." We aren't human without it, and we cannot live without it. However, our objective should be to heal our soul with love and acceptance. When we do, that voice settles down. If we continue to allow our soul to hold temper tantrums because it hates change, we will never truly hear God's voice, because He is in the gentle breeze, not the earthquake or hurricane-force winds. We are called to have dominion over the earth, not domination. The same is true with our soul. Be firm but kind.

Satan has just the opposite plan. He wants us to live in bondage. He will often feed lies to the soul to drown out our spirit. Feeling attacked? You will want to pray Jesus into your being and command Satan to leave. Claim your very being for God and work on listening more closely to your spirit. Our spirit is our partner and desires to make us free!

Ready to be FREE?

Speaking of freedom, we often decide to make a run for it when things go bad. We'll pick up and move to a new town, or we'll quit a career and start a new one. We literally run on empty and eventually crash and burn. Running away doesn't make us free, because we always show up! We can't outrun ourselves or God. F.R.E.E. stands for:

Forgiving ourselves and others;

Receiving God's message and direction;

Embracing our situations and circumstances;

Emulating the truth.

©LORRAINE BOSSÉ-SMITH

Forgiving others doesn't get them off the hook for what they have done to you; rather, forgiving them cleanses *your* soul of the pain. When you store up resentment and bitterness, you lose, not the offending party. Not forgiving someone is toxic to our body, and I firmly believe it causes illness inside of us. As the saying goes, when we don't forgive someone, we are drinking the poison expecting the other person to die! Each person has to reconcile his or her intents with their actual behaviors. Each person is responsible, but we must do our part of letting it go.

> *The path to hell is paved with good intentions.*
> ~ Saint Bernard of Clairvaux ~

Forgiving someone doesn't always mean reconciliation, either. I think churches mislead people into believing we must have a relationship with those we forgive. Not true! Our responsibility is to forgive, but we cannot make them actually change. That is between them and God. An abusive person can be forgiven, but you may need to distance or completely remove yourself from them in order to protect yourself from additional harm. Addicts may need to be entrusted into God's hand as you demonstrate tough love by walking away. You may not ever get an apology, but as long as *you* forgive, *you* can move on. What they do is their path, and they must walk it.

Forgiving ourselves is an entirely different story. If you are like me, this can take even longer. Our soul has a very long memory, and it reminds us of our failures and faults on a regular basis. This is why recognizing and acknowledging our spirit and connection to God is so vital. Our spirit brings goodness, hope, faith, and love to our weary soul. Our battered soul, along with negative forces working against us, can keep us in bondage. We believe it is right for things to be wrong. This couldn't be further from the truth! Unfortunately, if we let our soul dictate and drive, we will not be able to receive all God has to offer us. God wants us to forgive, heal, grow, and move on.

Move On!

I know I was pulling a huge U-Haul full of hate toward my ex for years. By doing so, I allowed him to control my feelings. Every time he would harass, belittle, or threaten me, I would go in a tail spin. Downward I would go. One day, I had enough. I decided to live out my faith. Did I trust God or not? If the answer was yes, then I needed to unhook my U-Haul, and drive away. I would not live in fear any longer. If my ex wanted to harm me, or worse kill me, then God would either (a) protect me if this wasn't His will; or (b) allow this to happen as part of His plan. Either way, I was a child of God. I would not fear this pathetic man any more. I had to forgive my ex for what he had done and accept my part of it—I *allowed* him to mistreat me. We train people on how to treat us, remember.

We train people on how to treat us.

A friend recently told me my generosity toward others was actually getting in the way of my own prosperity. Ouch! Unfortunately, this was true. I was so busy trying to help others be their best, I put aside *my* dreams. My ex was no different. I thought if I loved him enough, he would *want* to be a better man. Fact was, he didn't give a hoot. He was hateful, mean, and abusive; he had no motive to change because I put up with it.

Be gentle with yourself as you come to grips with your role in your past. We are all broken and trying to make sense of life. We do the best we can. Thankfully, God loves us even when we blow it. Do forgive, but don't forget the lessons learned. God pulls something good out of every single situation.

Quiet Your Mind

Once we forgive others and ourselves, we are in a better position to hear God's message, which can often get lost in the midst of our battles with bitterness. This requires quieting our minds, which is easier said than done. Our mind is designed to serve us, not enslave us. Unfortunately, many minds run rampant, controlling their humans. Technology hasn't helped this condition at all. People are addicted to social media sites and smartphones, all feeding the mind more hyperactivity. God is in the spaces, in the quiet, silent moments. In order to hear Him, we must make room.

Prayer should be active, like a two-way conversation. Most of us, however, talk at God and hardly take a second to listen for His reply. Meditation is a great way to settle down the soul and allow the spirit to connect with God. Yoga is one way of getting yourself to a good state, and my yoga program is: Yoking Ourselves to God Always (my *Yoga with Lorraine* DVD is available at my website: www.lorraine-bosse-smith.com/shop). However you quiet your mind, do it! You might be amazed at what God has to share with you.

After my ugly divorce and death of my mom, I had to find a job. I desperately wanted security. Companies from all over the country were calling me with decent offers. I had so many, I wasn't sure which one to take. In my quiet, reflective time, God gave me HIS direction. *Lorraine, you will find no security in a man, or a job for that matter. The only secure thing is Me.*

And with that, I was instructed to decline on ALL the job offers and start my own business. I never in a million years considered myself an entrepreneur, but God had other plans. These plans were confirmed by two phone calls to me with project work. They didn't know I was going on my own but thought I should, and they wanted to put their money where their mouths were. Within three days, I had a business name, cards, and two clients. Trust me, listening to God pays off! I have now been running my own business for over 18 years. Yes, God is good.

Embrace Your Situations

Difficult times are never easy to go through. During the pain, all we want is for it to stop. My experience is God often uses these trying times to get my attention, teach me a lesson, or point me in the right direction by closing doors.

As I have built my business (actually two through the years), my mission has been to simply improve the quality of people's lives through speaking, training, consulting, and writing books like this one. Through some awful experiences with people whom I invested in, trusted, and helped grow their business, God spoke loud and clear once again: *Dear one, improving the quality of people's lives shouldn't involve YOUR quality of life decreasing. I've never asked that of you, and never would.*

Sigh. I had done it again! I went down a path for the right reason but lost sight of my own wellbeing, security, and peace. Two people sucked the life out of me professionally and personally. The sad part was, I let them! Things came to a head, as they always will, and I realized, finally, I needed to break clean from these takers or vampires as I call them.

These situations were unpleasant, but ignoring them or running from them would not change the truth: I let vampires attach to me! When I faced my own mistakes of allowing them to mistreat me, take advantage of me, and screw me financially, I was able to embrace the pain. I could see the purpose God had through these circumstances. I still had to deal with them, but I could see past them. I knew better things awaited me on the other side.

Improve the Quality of YOUR Life

If you aren't happy with your life, look no further than the mirror. We are our own worst enemies, and we must stop following bad patterns. God's truth is a wonderful reminder of the good life He wishes for us. Take time to absorb it and apply it in your life. The awesome result is twofold. One, you will improve the quality of your own life. Two, you will be a light, an example to others that a better life is possible. Everyone wins!

The quality, not the longevity,
of one's life is what is important.
~ Martin Luther King, Jr.
~ MINISTER

DEFY YOUR DIAGNOSIS CHAPTER SEVEN

FIT Life Formula @ Work

Who has hurt you? Write out the top offenses, their name, and the relationship between you (use additional paper if necessary):

Using this list, acknowledge the pain, suffering, and effects these actions have had on your life:

Have you forgiven each person? Can you pray for them? (Note: Forgiving doesn't mean forgetting or minimizing what happened.)

If you have not forgiven a person, make a decision to do so. Write a letter to them sharing your feelings about how they hurt you and truly forgive them for their offense. (Note: You don't have to send the letter to them. This is for YOU, not them.)

CHAPTER EIGHT

Choose Relationships Wisely

Truth is everybody is going to hurt you:
you just gotta find the ones worth suffering for.
~ BOB MARLEY ~
Singer & Songwriter

I've mentioned already how I was married to an abusive man for six years. When asked why I stayed so long, my answer is complex due to my faith (told divorce is not permitted), insecurities, and warped belief I didn't deserve any better. The bottom line, however, is days turned into weeks; weeks turned into months; and months turned into years. In my spirit, I knew I was with the wrong man. My heart ached each day for better, but I did not take action. Friends and church leaders told me I had to accept the abuse as God's will. The sad part is how I took this as a truth, as do so many. What a tragedy! This is absolutely not what God has in mind for us. Divorce is not fun; it really does rip two lives apart. I can attest, though, how this painful process can be the best thing to do. Each person must decide for him or herself.

In my case, God Himself intervened on my behalf. He got my

attention with my mom's death. Once again, I was reminded how short life is, and I didn't want to spend another second with this brutal beast who abused me emotionally, mentally, spiritually, and physically. I can so relate with the Michael Bublé song "It's a Beautiful Day," in which he sings about how happy he is to NOT have this woman in his life! It's a catchy song, and I didn't really hear the words until recently. Yes, the sun was brighter and life richer *without* my ex in my life. Perhaps you can relate.

Since then, I have worked extremely hard to align myself with the right people. I'm not suggesting all the people in our lives need to look exactly like us, but we should have core principles in common. What matters to you may be different than me, and that is fine. But as you seek deep, intimate relationships with others, be sure they are worthy of your time, energy, and affection.

We Get What We Tolerate

I shared my concept of vampires earlier in this book as well as more in depth in my other book, *I Want My Life Back!* What I have since discovered, though, is decisions can come back to haunt us. You see, we are not the same person today as we were yesterday. Thank God, right? I pray I won't be the same person tomorrow as I am today. With God's help, I always want to improve and create a better version of myself. Our relationships tend to mirror our life and where we are on the journey. Those from our youth may not connect with us today—just depends upon the growth of the individuals. Being associated and aligned with the wrong people may not create stress early on, but as more time passes, along with personal development, the wider the gap. What once gave energy to your life will start to drain it and can cause you grief, pain, and even harm. I know I'm guilty of not letting go of friendships of days gone by I should have cut ties to long ago.

A long-term friend of mine, who was also a business associate of mine, began taking advantage of my generosity—to the degree where she took money for projects but did not do the work. I was left holding the bag several times. I had to do the work, but I did not get paid since my "friend" kept the money. Her behavior infuriated me, but when I was honest with myself, I was not surprised. I met her years ago when I was new to an area and desperately seeking friends. I hadn't come to grips with the "less is more" concept. She was smart and funny, but she was always late, self-absorbed, and flakey. We were opposites in about every way possible. I exercised to stay in shape, and she ate like a pig and got liposuction each year to remove all her excess fat. I didn't smoke or drink; she did like a sailor. I had my faith; she despised religion.

As time went on, she had an excuse for everything, and wasn't reliable one bit. Knowing this, I still proceeded to be her friend and offered her work. Because she was in a tight spot due to a divorce, I erroneously thought she would clean up her act and deliver work on time. She was broke and on the brink of being homeless. I thought I was helping her, but in reality, I was preventing her from dealing with HER stuff and hitting her own rock bottom. I got in the way of God's plan for her. I gave quality to her at the expense of mine, and she brought me nothing but hardship and stress.

I have no one to blame but myself for getting screwed! She behaved as she always had, and I tolerated it. I may have had good intentions, but I didn't stand up for myself. I didn't fight for what was right *for me*. Shame on me, and shame on you for your relationship messes. We get what we tolerate! We should not hate these people but instead be glad they taught us a valuable lesson: less **is** more.

Less Really Is More

As I reflect on this friendship, I see how one sided it truly was and how it didn't give me much, other than drama and stress. Every once in a while, she would send a funny e-card, but she did not call me or offer encouragement during any difficult time in my life. She was

Lorraine Bossé-Smith

absolutely, 100 percent focused on her own life and utterly selfish and self-centered. Although I tried to ask for favors and some mutual exchange of friendship, she gave none. Yet I continued the friendship. I basically trained her on how to treat me—like garbage! After cutting ties with her completely, I learned she had been lying since the day I met her, making up stories to gain sympathy. She has played many people, so I am not the only sucker. In addition, she is a drug addict. All I can hope is she falls hard and FINALLY faces herself. That is between her and God. I am just grateful for the lesson learned: a few quality friends beats a high volume of vampires!

How people treat you is their karma;
how you react is yours.
~ WAYNE DYER ~
Author

Clean House

Even though I am very deliberate about whom I connect with presently, I still have a few unhealthy long-term relationships. So I've embarked on cleaning my relationship house! With God's help, I plan on making room for the right people by getting rid of the wrong ones. We only have so much energy, and what a shame how we are spending valuable, priceless energy on people who really are not worth the effort.

Please don't misunderstand my motives here. I'm not elevating myself as so perfect that no one measures up. Rather, I am seeking quality. I am all about improving the quality of people's lives. I am a giver! I always look for how I can contribute. However, these relationships should not be at the expense of my own happiness, health, or quality. When so-called friends cannot be bothered to love you or reach out to you unless they need something, you need to evaluate

134

that friendship. Every relationship should be give and take, but if they are taking without making deposits, you may need to move on.

I've heard the saying how we are an accumulation of our five closest friends. Take a look around you and see what this is telling you. Only you can decide. This is your life.

Don't Believe the Lie

Social media has not served us well. Leonard Pitts, Jr. from the *Miami Herald* wrote an excellent piece on how technology has been anything but social. He used the example of a man waving a gun around on a packed commuter train back East. No one noticed—not a one. Everyone was too busy texting, surfing the internet, or Facebooking. Only when he finally shot a man dead did anyone look up. I don't know what they did, but I am sure many took pictures and posted it on their social media pages, which sickens me beyond words.

Do not buy into the lie of having 4,000 Facebook friends will make you happy. Those are not authentic relationships. They aren't even real friends, if you want to know the truth. Sure, some close friends will use social media to stay in touch with you, but the majority of folks are not active participants in your life. They are simply observers, liking how you had a rotten day.

Another friend of mine is addicted to social media. He has forgone his true friends, those who have loved him through some really tough times, and now spends all his time typing empty messages that are simply noise on his wall. He can't be bothered to reach out to a few loved ones because he is too busy with pleasing the masses. That is the lie. We have all gotten suckered into believing the world cares. Unfortunately, it does not. The world turns, regardless if your life is going great or in ruins. Kirk Douglas, actor, told his son, Michael Douglas, this, "If you can count your true friends on one hand, then you are blessed." I couldn't agree more! Life isn't about impressing others by blowhard postings without depth. Life is the simple moments shared with people who invest not their money but their time, energy, and love *in* us, and us in them.

Celebrate, Not Tolerate

Have you ever been so good at something people complain? "Hey, slow down. You are making the rest of us look bad!" I've heard comments like this my entire life, and for a long time, I deliberately tried not to outshine those around me. I carefully made sure I wasn't out doing anyone, not wanting to upset the apple cart. I held back. Well, no more! We all deserve to be around people who celebrate our gifts and talents. If the people you hang with are jealous, envious, or angry at what you have going on, you need a new group of friends. If you are constantly the smartest person in the room, you need a new group of friends.

A great exercise is to draw a large circle with circles within. Make as many layers are you want, but the smallest, inner circle is reserved for only those closest to you. You won't have hundreds here but rather a select few. The outer circle is Facebook and other social media. Yes, we know them, but our relationship is superficial. We have only surface-level discussions, posts, and interaction. We decide what they see and vice versa. In contrast, the inner circle is those you call in crisis, and they respond, not just "like" your posting.

Place the names of your friends and decide how far or close to the center they are presently. I was actually quite surprised at how many really were more toward the outside. I'm okay with just a handful of true friends. This doesn't mean I stop all contact with friends further out, but I do manage my expectations. I won't expect a lot, and I won't give a lot. Those who have chosen to be my dear friend (thank you!), commit to giving to me, and I to them.

Align with Like-Minded People

The bottom line is we should be aligning ourselves with those we have a deep connection with. If someone lies and you value honesty, why would you tolerate them? We often make the mistake of putting less weight to important issues, trying to be accommodating and accepting. Yes, we need to understand everyone is different. We should not judge. However, I caution you on allowing too many wolves in your sheep herd. Wolves eat sheep. They may be able to curb their appetite for a while, but eventually, their teeth come out; blood splatters. And when you are wounded and hurt, you let them in. They were only doing what they were born to do.

When dating, you must be very clear on what matters most to you. The heart can, and will, fall for the wrong person. Be sure you know yourself before you get seriously involved with someone. This sounds simple, but we often spend so much energy getting along with others (parents, sibling, co-workers, etc.) we can lose sight of what WE really like. Don't eat at a restaurant just because someone suggested it. Eat where YOU want to eat. See movies you enjoy. Life requires compromise, but the dating relationship is where you have the most freedom to explore. When and if you settle down with someone, you will have plenty of time to give and take. I encourage you to get my booklet *Dating with Style!,* which helps you understand your unique wiring and then how to identify others. Don't blindly go out but instead, date with style!

Dating with Style

I'm not talking about what you wear, although you should wear what makes you happy. I'm referring to our personality styles. We are all made different. You were born with a specific temperament, and all your life it has influenced everything you do. How you communicate, shop, eat, walk, exercise, manage your time, and drive are conducted in a manner that works for *you*. The trouble with dating is we often attempt to conceal our true identity. We desperately want to *fit* with someone. As a result, we may not be authentic and real with ourselves and the people we date. This is a recipe for disaster!

Most women I know spend more time considering who would manage their money than who they actually spend the rest of their lives with. If we aren't being honest about who we are, we will definitely miss who the other person is, and we may not be a match.

The old adage is correct most of the time: opposites attract. What you are lacking, the other person has and vice versa. This can create a most wonderful partnership. However, in order to have a great relationship, we must first look at *ourselves*. We are part of the couple. In fact, we are the only person in the relationship we can change. Hopefully, you have figured this out already and are ready to build a bridge to a happier, more fulfilling relationship, regardless of where it leads.

So ask yourself, Are you more outgoing, or reserved? If you are different at work, think of home life. Are you like a Jim Carrey, loving the spotlight, or are you happy being behind the scenes? Then ask yourself, Do you prefer checking things off of a list and getting things done, or do you always think of the people involved first? We are complex beings, and you will have to be both outgoing and reserved throughout your life; however, you feel more comfortable one way or the other. Select that one. Life will require you to be both task and people oriented, but your mind will go to one automatically. Pick that one.

If you selected outgoing and task oriented, you are an **Assertive Communicator** or a **FAST individual**, representing about 10 percent of the total population. You are a success-oriented, results-driven individual. Your communication style is direct and to the point. You don't like anything being forced or pushed upon you; you prefer to be in charge and make the decisions. Unless you ask for details, you lose interest in specifics quickly. You walk and talk fast! When stressed, you can become bossy and demanding.

If you selected outgoing but are more people oriented, you are an

Animated Communicator or **FUN person**, representing about 25–30 percent of the total population. Although you are also outgoing, your "Internal Compass" points you toward people. You are an interactive, expressive individual who wants to be popular and have fun. You enjoy the entire experience of being with people, but you can be easily distracted. You are high energy, but can often be disorganized. Details are not your bag! When stressed, you can have emotional outbursts, attack, and blame others.

Now, if you chose reserved with your people preference, then you are an **Attentive Communicator** or **FRIENDLY**, representing about 30–35 percent of the total population. You tend to be a quiet and shy individual. You require stability and avoid change of any kind if possible. You care deeply and want to help others. You move and speak much slower than the first two profiles. In fact, you are a fantastic listener! But, under pressure, you may go too far and withdraw, punishing people with the silent treatment.

And, if you chose reserved but are more task oriented, then you are an **Accurate Communicator** or **FACTUAL type**, representing about 20–25 percent of the total population. Although also reserved, your "Internal Compass" prefers tasks. You are a person of few words and are analytical by nature. You tend to take in everything and sift it through a screening device called logic. You prefer facts and figures to emotions. When under pressure, you can become very critical.

Remember, no one style is better than any other. You actually have all four temperaments in you, as does everyone. You prefer and typically operate from your primary or dominant style. The world needs all styles, and you have probably dated all of them! Ever wondered why some dates went smoothly and others were bumpy? We typically communicate in a manner that works for us, but it doesn't mean our communication works for others. Similarly, if your date doesn't even try to figure out your style, he or she will treat you as he or she wants to be treated. If you are the same style, you click. If you aren't, alarm bells sound.

The best thing you can do as you search for love is be true to your-self first and then honestly get to know your date. Ask questions and let them respond. Did they talk fast or slow? Did they use hand ges-tures or were they very conservative? These are all clues!

Disappointment is unmet expectations.
~ Brené Brown ~
Author

Living with the Love of Your Life

Even when we do our best to find just the right person, we aren't guaranteed an easy ride. Life throws us lots of curve balls. Mother Theresa was known for saying, "Love until it hurts." I cannot think of any relationship more suited for this statement than marriage. It requires us to give our all—and then some. The key is to give your spouse what he or she needs, not what works for you. As you have learned, these can be very different. Many a fight is a result of unmet expectations. We assumed our spouse thought and felt like us, and we, therefore, expected them to react just as we would.

If you align yourself with someone who has the same values, morals, beliefs, and a complementary style, you at least have a solid foundation. When the bombs are dropped, you have good chances of sustaining the damage and pressing forward. When life is going well, you'll feel as if you are floating. All your efforts spent to choose the right person will be well worth it.

Manners Still Matter

Whether with friends, family, or loved ones, when a conflict arises, be the first person to say, "I am sorry." Then, own up to what you did, and sincerely try to do better next time. Telling someone how sorry you are that *they* took what you said wrong is offensive. In essence, you are blaming the situation on them, when the reality is you are probably the culprit. Whether you are a man or woman, manner up!

Technology is a great tool, but we must always remember to keep it in its place. It is supposed to serve us, not enslave us. And, it should never trump people. Just as you wouldn't SCREAM at someone, do not use all caps in your email or IMs. Regardless of the technology, they are not the place to break up a marriage, split from your boyfriend, dump a girlfriend, or slander your former boss. Show some respect for others and yourself.

If someone invests their time, money, and heart into a gift for you, why wouldn't you want to tell them thank you? Send a note in the mail, which is the *least* you can do. Don't be a schmuck! All etiquette gurus agree on this point: Email is not sufficient. Email, of course, is better than nothing, but I challenge you to manner up and write a note. By the way, you have to actually mail the card!

I believe respect starts with us. When you show up to a store in your PJs, you have zero respect for yourself. Seriously? What kind of statement are you trying to make—too lazy to get dressed? Back in the day, people would dress in their Sunday best to travel. Now people fly in sweat pants. In the business world, experts tell us to dress for success, meaning wear appropriate clothing for the position you *want*, not your current job. Start dressing better when you run errands. When you do, you'll feel better abound yourself, and I bet you will treat others better as well.

Be courteous: When someone else is speaking, listen! Don't interrupt or step all over them. Wait your turn. Better yet, be an active listener and ask questions rather than jump into what you want to say. If we can all start mannering up, I believe we can shape up, creating an improved society, one we can all be proud of.

"Do unto others as you would have them do to you."
~ The Golden Rule ~

Invest Wisely

A big movement in the business world right now is getting the "right people, in the right seats on the right bus," writes Patrick Lencioni, author of *The Five Dysfunctions of a Team*. I believe it applies to our personal lives as well. Life is journey. Who do you want to travel with? Do you want negative people who bring you down or positive ones who lift you up? Life is too short to be with the wrong people. At work, we may feel we have to tolerate them, but in our personal life, we absolutely have a choice.

Ever been on a long flight and had a complainer sitting next to you? Everything went bad for them, and everyone mistreated them. They aren't happy about their seat, where they are going, and what they are doing. This makes for a very long flight! I'm not advocating being mean and "dumping" people in your life if they make a mistake. We all make mistakes and that is what grace is for. You know what I am talking about. The wrong people *for* you can be a cancer in your life. Life is too short! Cut the ties and move on.

Once you find the right people, you must start investing in them. Relationships should go both ways. Want a true friend? Be one!

Want a true friend … be one!

Just like we cannot write a check when our bank account is zero, we cannot expect people to give all the time to us. We must also invest in their lives. Certainly, none of us gives because we want to take—that is not our motive—but we should be making "deposits." What have you done lately for that special person who means so much to you? How have you shown a friend that you care? From your original list, please put the name of at least one from each category here that energize you. Rate how well you feel you have been developing this relationship (0 to 10 with 10 being excellent) and add what you plan to do to improve it:

Name	Category	Quality	Plan

Love that lasts involves a real and genuine concern
for others as persons, for their values as they feel them,
for their development and growth.
~ EVELYN DUVALL ~
Sociologist

Build a Foundation

Have you read the book *The Five Love Languages* by Gary Chapman? If you haven't, I encourage you to read it. He outlines the ways in which each of us prefers to be loved and supported. Just like we all have unique personalities, we all have different needs. Some of us prefer gifts while others need quality time. Others seek affirmation. Understanding the people in your life and what matters to them will build a solid foundation and allow you to invest in a manner that works. We certainly get points for trying, but when we nail it, we get huge points.

I love it when my husband does things for me: washes my car, fixes the lights in the garage, mows the grass, and dumps the garbage without me asking. These things make me happy. My husband, on the other hand, is thrilled when I show my appreciation to him. A compliment goes a long way for him. Well, during our first years of marriage, I was doing things for him, and he was complimenting my every move. We both felt unappreciated! Until we looked further at why, we felt the other party wasn't loving or thoughtful. That wasn't the case; we were both trying, but we were doing it in a way that worked for us. If you can uncover what makes your husband, children, family, and friends happy, then your gifts will mean so much more to *them*. Your relationships will be stronger and healthier.

Be Generous

Scarcity is a negative attitude. Read any of the financial success books, and they talk about how when we act and live like we don't have enough, we never will. Tithing is about that very thing. It helps us create an attitude of having plenty so that we may share with others. I see a tragic pattern in society. People are living like they don't have enough time, enough energy, or enough love to go around, so they retreat and do for "theirs." They can't be bothered with others. I see it with parents of young kids; they can't possible do anything but raise their kids. Hmmm … how did our mothers do it then? I see it in women who have big, high-paying corporate jobs. They feel they work too much and can't do anything else. What is happening, sadly enough, is that society is creating this reality.

When we think only of ourselves and don't reach out, the world becomes a cold and unfriendly place. Everyone begins to feels the scarcity and retreats further. It's a vicious cycle. I encourage you to be generous with your smiles and laughs. These are free but can make you and others feel so much better. Be giving with compliments and courtesies like please and thank you. These don't take much effort but can establish a positive rapport immediately. Be patient and kind. We will always get further with sugar than salt. Be available. Taking everything we have discussed into account, we still need to be available for the situations God presents to us.

> *When one door closes, another opens. But we often look*
> *so long and so regretfully upon the closed door that*
> *we do not see the one which has been opened for us.*
> ~ HELEN KELLER ~
> *Author*

In fact, if we are managing our time, emotions, mind, and relationships, we will have the time, energy, and desire to reach out, help, and serve.

Create a Healthy Home

And don't forget to serve your family. In some cases, we can go so extreme at being available to the world that we forget our very own family. Home is a place for the entire family to feel loved and safe. It is our refuge. The responsibility falls on women's shoulders to create a safe haven for their families, regardless of whether they work outside of the home or not. This isn't implying that men don't do anything around the house, but it is right in line with our biblical role of help-mate. We are the sensitive and caring ones. This should be our job. And because I know how hard this job can be, I have offered ways to help you reduce your stress, become more balanced, and feel happier. The saying is oh so true: when Mama ain't happy, no one is happy! We have that kind of influence over our families, and we need to take it seriously. We need to monitor ourselves. Let me ask you a few questions: 1) Are you edgy? 2) Are you overly critical? 3) Are you annoyed, angry, and upset most of the time? This book came at the right time then! If you aren't on the brink of burn out, I'm glad. This book will help you stay that way.

Start journaling. I know you have probably done journaling in the past, but I want you to change how you do it. I want it to be a **Joy Journal**. I want you to start concentrating on what is wonderful about your spouse and family, not what is driving you crazy. By doing this, you will change your attitude and create a more positive environment for everyone.

And don't forget your pets! Pets truly love us unconditionally. They don't care what we look like or what we own. Children who are raised with animals are much more adjusted, confident, and healthy.

Keep the Flame Going

One word of caution: Don't let your pet replace your spouse. When research studies find that most women would choose their pet over their husband if stranded on a deserted island, we have gone overboard with our pets. I thank God for my cat and dog. They are so special to me. I know at times my husband can feel third in line to them. How awful of me! The reality SHOULD be that our spouses are first. Our pets add to our partnership and family. We need to treat our spouses as well as we do our beloved animals … hopefully even better.

What turns your mate on? What rocks his or her boat? Save enough of yourself to give to your mate. Life will always present challenges. We have to maintain, nurture, develop, and grow our relationships *despite* what is going on. I think we can be guilty of putting our husbands on hold until "things settle down." All of a sudden, the years have gone by, and we look at our spouse and go, "Now who are you?" Don't let this happen. I've seen it in other marriages, and it is tough to rebound … not impossible, but tough.

What kinds of things would make your spouse smile? Jot a list of them down right here and then commit to one a week for a month.

MY HONEY DO LIST

_____ _____

_____ _____

_____ _____

_____ _____

_____ _____

The amount of satisfaction you get from life
Depends largely on your own ingenuity, self-sufficiency, and
resourcefulness. People who wait around for life to supplyt
heir satisfactions usually find boredom instead.
~ Dr. William Menninger ~
American psychiatrist

Live Life to the Fullest

Relationships are ever changing. A dear friend says that they are like an onion. When you peel one layer off, you have another layer.

We will constantly be learning and growing, and that means we are alive. Celebrate your victories and learn from your mistakes because that is really all any of us can do. The good news, I hope, is that you have more tools now to help improve your relationships. As you apply them, your quality of life will go up, and your stress will go down. I'm rooting for you!

DEFY YOUR DIAGNOSIS CHAPTER EIGHT

FIT Life Formula @ Work

What vampiric relationships are negatively impacting your life?

Why have you chosen to tolerate the abuse, neglect, or one-sided relationship?

Do you feel you are co-dependent (inability to set healthy boundaries)? If so, what steps are you going to take to create healthier relationships moving forward?

CHAPTER NINE

Listen For God's Whisper

Don't let the doubts of others ring louder than
God's whisper to your spirit.
~ TRICIA GOYER ~
Author

I love the passage in the Bible about how God did not come in the storm, the wind, or in an earthquake. No, God came in a gentle whisper (see 1 Kings 19:11–12). I know in my life when I have sought the Father, He has always come quietly into my heart, especially when I am out in His countryside.

Pay Attention

On one such outing, the wind was whipping through the rugged trees and rocky terrain, yet the sun glistened as to kiss the powder blue Colorado Rocky Mountain sky. I love these kinds of days, hiking in God's beautiful canvas. Up here, about 11,000 feet above sea level, I belonged. The rat race of my life below seemed distant and but a mere image fading further away with every gust. I could be myself, let go, relax, and reflect.

I'll never forget the year when my life unraveled before my very eyes. The tapestry so carefully sewn together through time seemed to disintegrate and explode. I found myself without things I thought were important and losing ones that really were. Hiking was therapy for me—a chance to talk with God.

On this particular day, He brought me to a special area. As usual, my small mind thought He was blessing me with the chance to admire the scenery. Oh, it was beautiful all right, but God had much more in mind for me.

High above civilization, I found these trees. They were the weirdest things I had ever seen in my life! I remember my brother explaining how they were one of the oldest species of trees in existence. They made their home—a place where most trees would not dare—where the conditions were harsh and the weather extreme. At first glance, they seemed to be nothing more than a twisted tree, mangled to the point of deformity. I'm sure many people just pass them by without a glance as they use their binoculars to view the breathtaking scenery around. I might have also overlooked them, but on this particular day, I would see them for their true beauty.

Be a Bristlecone

Be like a bristlecone pine tree, God's spirit moved in my heart. I looked closer at these trees, and I began to realize for the first time they were not twisted because God had made a mistake in their creation. God doesn't make mistakes. No, they were uniquely designed because they were flexible. Wind is inevitable. We can't avoid it in our lives either—it *will* come. Sometimes it is a slight, warming breeze that sooths the soul while other times, it whips through, howling at forceful speeds. It can knock down even the biggest, widest tree in a flash, as if it were merely a twig in the ground. But instead of fighting the wind, the bristlecone pine tree bends and moves with the wind. Each tree, therefore, has a very unique shape formed by and determined by the winds in which it sustained.

Things are not always what they appear to be. I sat and reflected on this statement. How many times have I assumed a tree, a cactus, or whatever was ugly just because it didn't look like everything else when it merely was an example of how it actively persevered life's challenges? Was I making the same judgment to people whose appearance or lifestyle was different than mine?

Have Faith

Have faith like a bristlecone pine tree was whispered in to my spirit next. Flexibility alone wasn't the answer. The other quality helping these trees live very long lives is the fact they have one of the deepest root systems. Instead of settling for the quick, easy surface water, the bristlecone pine tree goes deep down into the core of the ground. When the droughts come, and we know they will, it is prepared. These trees need not worry or dread, because they do not rely on the water that comes and goes daily.

How deep were my roots? Deep enough to withstand a drought? Well, I was in one! The ground was cracking, and the plant life was drying up and blowing away. Yet I was *still* standing. Oh sure, I didn't look the same as before. Maybe to some, I appeared a bit mangled. But, as I stood admiring these gorgeous creations of God, I was filled with a heart of thankfulness and gratitude. What a lesson these trees are for us all.

As I have shared this with some, they exclaimed, "No way. I rather be a big, tall, huge redwood (sequoia) tree so everyone can see me and know I stand for God." Well, that may be their desire, but I rather proudly consider myself a bristlecone pine tree—uniquely designed and deeply rooted. When people see me, they won't just say, "Wow, what a big tree." No, they will look a little closer to learn what and who has made me.

Listen for God's Whispers

God often uses quiet moments in our life to speak to us if we will just listen. I love the word *whisper* so much I created an acronym:

Worship with Him

Hope for Our Questions

Insight/Guidance for Our Lives

Special People in Our Lives

Peace through Prayer

Encouragement for the Day

Rest in Him

Worship

Nature itself is a symphony God has written for Himself. The heavens declare His handiwork (Psalm 19:1), and we get to enjoy it all! Worship is more than just something done in church and set to music. Worship is intended to be exhibited in everything we do and say, indeed, in everything we are. Yet Christ said true worship starts in the heart. This is the kind of worship the Father is seeking. If we can keep our focus on *who* God is and what He has done, we can turn worship into a continuous exchange of gratitude to Him.

Worship is communion with God. This is our opportunity to pour our heart and soul out. Music is such a gift, and it can lift a weary soul up or fill one with God's Holy Spirit.

Father, may everything we do be done with You in mind.
May our hearts be truly devoted to You.
Let our voices and actions please You.
Amen.

Hope

Ever have something happen to you, and you find yourself asking God why? Now in answering this question, you either: lied, gave a hearty amen, or you've been living in a cave and this is the first trip you've had into civilization! Human nature is to ask why.

The writer of Hebrews tells us faith is being sure of what we hope for and certain of what we do not see (11:1). I've seen quite a few things I didn't understand. My family lost a father and husband to cancer when I was thirteen. Why? God could have healed him but chose to welcome him home instead. I may never know why, and I had to come to terms with that truth. Faith comes in accepting those things we don't know or understand. Hope comes in knowing our heavenly Father knows best.

Prayer is a wonderful way for us to remember God cares for us, hurts with us, and cries along side of us. We are not alone.

Abba Father, thank you we are not alone in the tough times.
You've promised to never leave us nor forsake us.
You're right here with us, and more importantly,
You'll be with us when this is over.
Help us to always hope in Your promises.
Amen.

Insight

"If any of you lacks wisdom, he should ask God, who gives generously to all without finding fault, and it will be given to him" (James 1:5). That's great news! God will give us wisdom, but we have to actually apply this wisdom to benefit from it.

Sometimes we want answers on large scales. *God, what should I do with my life?*

He usually replies in smaller tones. Be bolder today; spend more time with Him now.

Share His love with all you encounter! When He gives short-term answers, we must have more faith to follow Him.

God's Word is truly a light unto our path. It gives just enough light so we don't stumble over what's immediately in front of us or cause shadows of doubt to creep over the trail ahead.

God, show us the steps You've already ordained for us
to walk on the path You have for us.
Let us walk where You lead,
then we'll know You've already gone before us.
Amen.

Special People

Adam needed Eve. Jesus needed Peter, James, and John, though arguably the latter three got much more out of it than Jesus did. You and I need people, too. They make us who we are. They know how we really are, and God allows them to love us anyway. What a gift! They are the special people in each of our lives, those we couldn't live without.

Family, friends, teachers, pastors … God has chosen people for each of us to show His love to us and for us to show His love to them. He gives us special people to encourage and uplift us, to allow us to bear the burdens of others, and also to lighten our load on both fronts.

Father, as iron sharpens iron, so you've placed people in our life to help
mold us into what You want us to be. Help us to be able to help others,
too. Don't let us take these great blessings for granted.
Amen.

Peace

Imagine your family faces a decision that could cost one of its members their lives. Not making the decision will definitely shorten that life. What do you do? More importantly, what do you do after you've made that decision, and you wait to see how it turns out?

My mother was diagnosed with a brain tumor in 1997. Surgery would most likely leave her paralyzed but might offer a few more months of life. Without the surgery or God's intervention, doctors believed she would die within the year. We all agreed, and did not put Mom through the additional suffering. She died five short months later.

What helped me through this time was praying. Philippians 4 instructs us not to worry, and Paul gives a list of better things to let occupy our minds. Peace CAN be found in the midst of what seems to be our darkest night.

Lord, help us to see that You are in control. You calmed the stormy seas, and You can calm our troubled mind. Help us to think on those things that are good and lovely. Thank You for Your peace that surpasses our understanding.
Amen.

Encouragement

Someone once said they could go a whole week on a compliment. Psychologists say people need about twelve hugs a day for peak emotional health. The wisest man who ever lived, Solomon, said a word fitly spoken was like apples of gold in settings of silver. Now, that's some precious metal!

A kind word, a hug, or a pat on the back all say the same thing: Someone else noticed something about you. Not only did they notice, but they cared enough to let you know they noticed. Having noticed, they took the occasion to say they cared. People appreciate knowing you care more than what you know.

When you give encouragement, you are blessing others. When you receive it, savor it because we will always encounter those who rather put you down than pick you up. Thankfully, God uses those special people to breathe life into us.

God, you've given us wings. May we know when to fly!
Amen.

Rest in Him

The first week ended with a day of inactivity. The Creator rested in order for us to see how important it is. He knew it would not be easy. In fact, in Matthew 11, Jesus, says to come and learn how to rest in Him.

For all the ministry He did and could have done, Christ rested. He set time apart from people, often using it for prayer. If we will learn from Him, Jesus will teach us when to rest (probably more often than we do), where to rest (apart from potential distractions, good or bad), and He will show us how to rest (spending time in fellowship with the Father).

I've had to learn how to be still; it takes work. But the reward is great. God often waits for us to quiet our minds before He speaks. He wants our full attention so we don't miss all He has for us.

Lord, teach us to rest in You. Show us how to rest,
where to rest, and when to rest. Fill us up with Your peace.
Amen.

Breathe

May you make time to be still and know He is God. May you be keenly aware of His love and hear His words for you! May His whisper sooth your soul, lift your spirits, and fill your cup! Take the time to quiet your mind and receive. I've found yoga and meditation are wonderful tools for clearing out the garage cluttering our minds. Breathe in for a count of ten seconds, and then hold your breath for ten seconds, followed by exhaling for ten seconds. Repeat. Add your arms if you like, bringing them up with the inhale, palms together when you hold, and lower your arms on the exhale.

DEFY YOUR DIAGNOSIS CHAPTER NINE

FIT Life Formula @ Work

When was the last time you were quiet and still? Take some time this week to BE with God and listen for his whisper.

Who are the special people in your life? Take a moment to write their name down. Say a prayer for them. Better yet, reach out to them and thank them for being a part of your life.

Peace comes from putting our focus on what we have, not focusing on what we don't have. List at leave five things are you grateful for and praise God for them!

What tree or plant would describe you and your life best? Why?

CHAPTER TEN

Look For Lessons

Your time is limited, so don't waste it
living someone else's life.
~ STEVE JOBS ~
Co-Founder of Apple Computers

I picked up rock climbing since marrying my husband, Steve, who has been an enthusiast for many years now. A friend of ours, who is actually listed in climbing books, was kind enough to give us a refresher course in climbing safety. Knowing people have indeed died participating in this sport, I greatly appreciated the briefing. The first thing out of his mouth: "Trust the rope." The information that followed (how to tie a proper, secure knot followed by clipping in, adjusting your harness, etc.) was coming all at once. I tried to absorb as much as possible, but not until later would I truly understand the meaning of his first words.

Take a Chance

You may not rock climb, but you have seen it in movies or in TV commercials. Rock climbing is used for many motivational posters, signifying reaching the top. Some folks wonder why in the world anyone in their right mind would attempt to climb up a rock with their bare hands. Others simply say, "It's too dangerous." Yes, rock climbing has its risks just like everything else. A person has a greater chance of being in an automobile accident than they do falling off a rock. The incidents making the news are often cases of young, inexperienced people who didn't follow the basic rules that ALL climbers should follow, no matter their level of ability or years of experience. Most tragic mishaps involve alcohol and impaired judgment. Don't like risk? Chances are you are taking your own risks, especially if you are an entrepreneur. Like me, you have decided the benefits outweigh the risks. Or, you are willing to take the risks in hopes of obtaining something great. Either way, you calculate and assess your risks and carefully take them.

Contrary to popular belief, rock climbing is not haphazard. It is a very strategic and thoughtful sport, thus why I have enjoyed it immensely. It is not rushed or hurried. I have enough crazy things in my life! No, rock climbing is slow and sure, but it does have its risks. By following safety guidelines, a climber reduces his or her chances of a fall or injury. The more I climb, the more I realize these principles apply to our lives. Here is what I learned:

Trust Your Rope

I mentioned this earlier and learned how significant it was when I slipped during one of my earlier climbs. I went swinging across the rock. A climber must know his or her rope is strong. To ensure this, therefore, before each and every climb, the rope is inspected. A log is kept on the rope of the number of falls. Each rope is able to sustain a certain number of falls. When a rope has reached its limit, it is retired. In your life or business, you must trust God. He is your lifeline. He is the one who gave you your gifts and talents. He is the one who brought you to this place and, most likely, encouraged you to take the scary step of entrepreneurship or whatever. Be smart about your moves, but know if you fall, God *will* catch you. Without this trust, you will be a timid climber and won't reach the top.

Secure Your Equipment

A climber always ensures his or her carabineer or clip is "out and locked" and his or her harness is tight. A climber cannot skimp on equipment and must know it is solid. We can be tempted to skip steps and go skinny on essentials required for success, but we must remember our neck is on the line. You don't have to spend a fortune, but you will have to invest in yourself and your goals in order to move ahead. Good job on investing in this book!

Communicate

Climbing is mostly done in at least pairs. One person stands firmly on the ground and belays the rope, while the other person climbs up the rock. A climber never leaves the ground without first communicating his intent to his partner. Throughout the entire climb, both parties are talking: "Rock falling, handhold to your left, slack, break, climbing on," etc. Regardless of your dream and who it involves, you must communicate in order to succeed. Your written goal statement is your first voice. It expresses what you want to do, where you want to go and how you will get there. Each and every opportunity you have to share your dream with others becomes confirmation of what it is you do and clarified how you will do it.

Plan YOUR Route

Another element of rock climbing I enjoy is that it is very personalized. Two people can approach the same face but climb different routes based upon their ability. A climber must create his or her own route up the face. To reduce fatigue and frustration, a wise climber scouts out as much of his route before putting a hand on the rock. In life, if you do not have a clear vision of where you are going, you will end up creating frustration and pain for yourself and others. You will experience disappointment and waste your valuable time and money. When you create a plan, you know exactly where your next "hold" is and are ready to make the move.

Be Flexible

A climber must be flexible in more ways than one. Physical flexibility allows climbers to reach, stretch, and contort their bodies in any way necessary to move higher up the rock, but a climber also needs mental flexibility. Just because they planned a certain route doesn't mean the mountain will let them get to the top. Climbers must creatively come up with a Plan B on the spot. Be specific with your dream but also be flexible. Work your plan, but have an open mind for when things change. Remember, the goal is to get to the top; how you arrive doesn't really matter, does it?

Know When to Call It

Rock climbing is often used for motivational prints, portraying "getting to the top" when the real goal for climbers is a clean climb. How interesting! This does not always mean getting to the mountaintop but may mean getting to your top. I'm a high achiever who loves setting and achieving goals. I found this concept refreshing. "You mean I don't have to make it to the top?" I asked my friend. "Only if your ability will let you," he replied. Every climber is different, so one person may not be able to get to the mountaintop, but they can climb well with no falls (clean) and go as far as they can. This is a victory. Climbers must acknowledge their ability level and know when to call it, though. We all face a fine line: When do we keep trying, and when do we call it quits? Constantly monitoring your progress and being brutally honest with yourself will help you to make tough decisions.

And, I think we get too focused on big wins and lose site of the small successes; don't forget to celebrate, which brings me to my last lesson from climbing.

Celebrate Your Successes!

Rock climbing is physically and mentally exhausting. When we go out climbing, we are completely spent after about five climbs each. Our bodies are fatigued, and our brains mush. What a feeling to look down at what you have just conquered: 40 feet, 100 feet, or wherever you end up. Remember to pause long enough to reflect on how far you went and smile about what you have accomplished. If you don't, you may forget why you pursued your dream in the first place. For a rock climber, pushing their body hard, overcoming fear, and giving their best are rewarded with breathtaking views, fresh air, and a surreal moment of, "I did it."

Climb YOUR Mountain!

What Tennis Has Taught Me about Life

I have also enjoyed playing tennis since my youth. It is a great game of physical ability and mental strategy—one that can be played well into our golden years. Over the years, I have realized how very similar the game of tennis is to life. Here is what tennis has taught me about life:

1. How we play the game is **everything**. Tennis is one of those games where the final score may not really reflect the level of play. A score of 6–4 seems like a nice win, but each of those games could have gone to deuce several times, with one person finally pulling through or the other making a critical mistake. And although the score may not show how close each game was, your character was built, and so was your confidence. Consistently hitting the

balls back, determining to stay in the game no matter what, and staying with it to the very end is a win of itself.

2. We can't play alone. Although you can hit a tennis ball against the wall, that isn't near as fun as playing an opponent. In life and the world of business, as much as we wish our competitors did not exist, these adversaries force us to be at the top of our game. Why do professional tennis players who have mastered the skill continue to practice? Because they know someone else could beat them. This drives them to continually improve. We need healthy competition to keep our edge.

3. We need the right equipment. You can't play tennis with a baseball bat. Don't expect to achieve your goals if you aren't investing in the right tools, such as training and coaching. The most expensive gear isn't always the best, so be sure to match your needs to the proper equipment.

4. Don't play with mean people and choose your partner wisely. Mean people do suck, as the bumper sticker says. Life is *way* too short to be surrounded by grumps. Select the right partner, and you will soar. Pair up with a turkey, and you will spiral down. Don't waste energy on trying to make miserable people happy. Instead, take those positive people and invest in them. You'll have a much higher return on investment (ROI).

5. Leave the temper tantrums to John McEnroe (or whoever the latest, greatest athlete is with anger issues). When things don't go your way, don't explode. You lose face and expend priceless energy. No one is impressed with emotional outbursts. If you must release the tension, hit a tennis ball, just not directly at someone!

6. Double faults happen. Even with the best strategy and execution of a plan, things can go wrong. Anytime people are involved (when are they not?), errors can happen. Understand this

principle and save yourself a lot of grief. Focus on the solution rather than the challenge and look for ways to prevent it in the future. Beating oneself up over a bad shot just guarantees worse shots will come. Look at correcting the grip, swing, or position of the body, and see the improvements come.

7. Play hard! If you aren't going to give it your best, then why bother? Keep your eye on the ball at all times, be flexible, have a firm grip, and swing with purpose. Here's to being a champion! Tennis anyone?

"This is a test of the Emergency Broadcast System.
If this had this been an actual emergency, we'd all be dead!"

Life's Tests

Life is full of tests. Hopefully, we won't have to face such a dramatic, devastating test in our lifetime as the Emergency Broadcast System announcing a worldwide tragedy, but if we think we completed our education when we graduated from school (whatever level or grade), we have a rude awakening ahead of us. In reality, our learning has just begun!

The problem with the word *test* is we tend to have a negative association with it. Let's face it, we cringe at the word and thought of taking a test. I'm not talking about going down to your local DMV and taking a driving test, although if you move to California, you'd better study! The most obscure questions you can think of have absolutely nothing to do with your driving ability will be asked ... guaranteed. What I'm referring to here is "life tests." You know what I mean—those times in life when our patience or our faith is tested. Something blind sides us or takes us by surprise, and we find ourselves faced with a situation we must endure. I think we like these tests even less.

Another problem with "tests" is we as humans lose sight of the purpose of any test. Tests were designed and are used to measure our intelligence, personality, emotional well-being, and our behavior. However, we get lost in the score or grade. Our competitive side and our pride step in to ensure we pass and uphold a high GPA. We seem to forget the outcome was to learn more about the subject or ourselves.

Let's take one. I know I just confirmed how taking a test is like having teeth pulled, but bear with me. It's short on length but long on insight. Ready? You have a minute to complete the following questionnaire, and no cheating by looking them up!

1) What is the exact date of Jesus Christ's return?

2) How old is Larry King anyway?

3) How many strokes of paint did it take to paint the room you are sitting in? (Humor me, if you are in a room with wallpaper, image the paint underneath!)

4) What is my mother's maiden name?

Okay, did you know the answers to every question? Did you pass with flying colors? I'm not a betting kind of a person, but I would put money down to say no one got them all right, not even me, and I drafted up the questions! If this test applied toward our GPA, we'd all be in trouble. But you know what, every test we take applies to our GPA, but it isn't what and how you think.

I've decided GPA stands for our Godly Performance Average. Unlike college, the test score isn't what is calculated. No, *how* we handle the test, regardless of the score or outcome, is what matters. See, the fact is life will bring you some lemons. God isn't sitting up in heaven with His finger pointing down at people to determine who will suffer today, but every person has been given the free will to make choices. As we know, every choice we make has consequences. Sometimes, we even face unpleasant times due to someone else's bad judgment.

The bottom line: what will you do with it and how will you handle it? That's the point and is what God is watching, not the score.

Could you imagine if He *did* keep score of our GPA? I can only speak for myself, but I'd never graduate to heaven. I'd be permanently in summer school. Thankfully, God's tests are designed to help us grow, mature, and blossom. He wants us to succeed and pass. Even though we think we have failed or flunked a test, God is using it. Today's tests prepare us for tomorrow's challenges. You can bet we will have more tests. Don't set yourself up for disappointment. No one is immune to trouble. This is a fallen world. Until we get on the other side, we *will* face obstacles.

When they come, what or whom do you cling to? When things go sour or appear to be unraveling before your very eyes, do you focus on the problem or look for the positive end result? We must remember we have hope and encouragement in our trials. They are not just needless tests by God for us to be tortured or beaten down. Our Creator is loving and kind. Our circumstances allow God to mold us into an image more like Him, and our challenges become learning opportunities for us to embrace and to improve our GPA (Godly Performance Average).

Without hard work, nothing grows but weeds.
~ GORDON B. HINCKLEY ~
American religious leader and author

Weeding Isn't for Wimps

Speaking of challenges, weeds are a thorn in my side. I wish we would all declare weeds pretty and beautiful. I believe if we decided to adore them, they would wither and die. The other plants would, therefore, thrive. One Saturday morning I began my normal ritual of weekend chores: washing/folding clothes, watering plants, straightening up the house, cleaning the car, and weeding. I always dreamed of living in California, and my dream came true when my husband and I purchased a home after getting married. Ah, paradise! I quickly learned one of its drawbacks: no winter. Don't misunderstand me. I loved how every day was warm and sunny with blue skies. I didn't miss "winter" in the sense of coldness and harshness. I did miss the break from yard work, though. In California, the growing season is *all* year long. This sounds wonderful in relation to bushes, trees, and flowers, but it is a chore in relation to mowing the grass and pulling the weeds. Then we moved to Texas. My land! Things grew twice as fast. I swear, I could start at one end of the yard, and by the time I looked back to where I began, more weeds grew up!

When I weed, I put my gloves on and grab my weeding bucket. I then head out to face the challenge ahead. I hate weeding, I really do. They invade my lovely garden and threaten to destroy healthy plants. We have a good-size yard, and the weeds have plenty of opportunity and space to grow—and boy, do they! I have been amazed and literally astonished at times at the durability, toughness, and determination these weeds have. They are masters at maximizing the tiniest space, moving in, and claiming it as home. They are professional illusionists, hiding themselves in the midst of flowering plants. If I didn't know better, I would think they were waging war on me!

I consider myself to be in excellent physical and mental health. I work out five to six days a week. I read uplifting, positive, and inspiring works. Yet I don't often feel equipped for the weeding battle. My back gets sore; the back of my legs tighten; sweat drips down into my eyes; dirt accumulates under my nails; my arms and hands get tired; and I grow weary. As I continued wrestling with, yanking at, pulling on, digging up, and prying out these vicious weeds from the ground, I concluded, "Weeding is definitely NOT for wimps!"

But without the process, our yard would turn from beauty to disgrace; from order to chaos; and from peace to stress. Weeding is a necessary part of "homeowner's" life, and as I stood up pausing for a quick break (God has a way of speaking to us in the most unusual places), I reflected on how weeding applies to *all* aspects of our life. If we truly want to be healthy, we must take great care in tending our emotional, physical, and spiritual gardens.

I realized the nicest, most well-kept yard has an occasional weed invasion, and so does our life. In fact, our lives are full of many kinds of weeds. God never promised us a rose garden free of thorns or weeds. Life can be, and usually is, challenging. M. Scott Peck, in his book *The Road Less Traveled,* says "Life is difficult." Period. "The sooner we acknowledge and accept this truth, the quicker life is less challenging." Trials and tribulations are par for course.

Covered in dirt and sweat from head to toe, I surveyed my surroundings. I had pulled four types of weeds, and I believe these are the ones we battle the most in our own lives:

Shallow but smothering. These weeds are easily pulled out because their roots do not go deep. The challenge is finding the entire weed! They spread out and grow over the healthy plants. Left alone, they begin smothering the plant from the top down.

Beautiful but overbearing. These weeds are deceiving because their bright-colored blossoms appear to be lovely. But take a closer look, and they are taking over large areas of your garden. If left unattended, they will overpower your garden, and eventually healthy plants will be unable to grow.

Wide and wicked. These weeds are big and bad. They cover the ground and spread about until they dominate the plants around them. Their roots are thick, embedding them firmly into the soil. They are a pain to extract.

Deep and deadly. These weeds may not be seen on the surface. They tend to be small and unobtrusive, but don't let their size fool you. Their roots go literally a foot or more down into the tough, solid ground, preventing complete extraction. They are stubborn, strong, and difficult to kill.

If you are like me, you can feel discouraged and defeated as you glance over at all the weeds that have crept in and invaded your life. We can feel weary and weak just thinking of the work ahead of us, but we have great hope. God has given us excellent tools and equipment to combat, conquer, and kill our weeds. We just have to be willing to get a little dirty, and we must have courage. Weeding is definitely not for the faint of heart. It will indeed be hard work, but you won't regret the beautiful green, lush garden that will flourish. You have to be prepared to yank, pull, tug, dig, pry, spray, stomp, and destroy those unwanted weeds. So grab your gloves and slap on some sunscreen. Let's weed!

1. Look at your life for things taking or getting priority that really shouldn't. Too much television or Facebook? Too much food or alcohol? What about work? Are you giving more of yourself to your employer than to your loved ones and your relationship with God? Warning signs: bad attitude and negative thinking. Feeling overwhelmed and hopeless often. Get back on track. Put first things first.

2. Giving should be a priority. Our service to others is a reflection of our love for Him—meaning, the more we comprehend the gift, the more thankful we are, and the greater our desire to give back. Be careful, though, to serve for the right reasons and to set appropriate boundaries. Burnout can strike the most well-intentioned, God-fearing people. Warning signs: Feelings of resentment when serving. Saying yes when you really mean no. Exhaustion, tiredness, and irritability. Take inventory of your commitments and make sure you are where you really need to be.

3. On a bit more serious note, we can usually identify the problem but have difficulty changing it. They have been become a habit or pattern such as a flaring temper, stretching the truth, or gossiping. We can hardly remember a time when we didn't display this type of behavior. Warning signs: Not fellowshipping with others

or going overboard with commitments as a cover up. Talking a lot of talk but rarely walking it. Take action and take it now! Seek someone older and wiser and ask him or her to be your accountability partner. Pray for God's forgiveness and His power and strength to fill you up.

4. Behaviors have turned to addictions and abuse. No longer are they surface issues, but they have rooted themselves deep into the core of our being, putting all goodness in our life at risk. This is the red zone and calls for emergency help and drastic measures. Warning signs: Continually on the defense to loved ones. Denial of inappropriate behavior and resentment of subsequent consequences to actions. Resistance to help. Drop to your knees and ask the Holy Spirit to intervene. Join a recovery group. Start seeing a counselor on a regular basis and confess. Pray without ceasing.

Are we destined to lose the battle of the weeds? No! As with real weeding, it takes work, but with some regular attention, care, and persistent effort, our gardens can be greener, lusher, and enjoyable. Most importantly, they can be a reflection of the ultimate Gardener, Jesus Christ. Weed and weed often!

Life IS a Lesson

All of life offers the opportunity for us to grow and become better human beings. Without obstacles to overcome, we'd never learn to leap! Without roadblocks, we would never turn down a different road to discover what it has for us. Without delays, we wouldn't gain the ability to trust. Without hurts and disappointments, we would take good for granted. We need dark to appreciate the light.

I don't know what is going on in your life right now, but I can say with certainly you will be a different person tomorrow as a result. Whether that person is bitter or better is up to you.

DEFY YOUR DIAGNOSIS CHAPTER TEN

FIT Life Formula @ Work

What lessons has God taught you this month?

When life challenges or tests you, what is your first response?

Have you allowed weeds to grow in your spiritual garden? What kinds?

Seek the Father for strength to pull your weeds and write out a couple of your favorite, encouraging Bible verses here:

CHAPTER ELEVEN

Have A Sense of Humor

Life is hard. After all, it kills you.
~ Katherine Hepburn ~
Actress

Life with my husband, Steve, has been a great adventure. We've been blessed to live in some incredible places: the Central Coast of California, Southern California, Colorado, and now Arizona. We were living north of Denver when my husband informed me that he received a job offer from Houston, Texas. I knew he was ready for the next step up on the corporate ladder, but I had hopes of heading back to California or to Arizona. We are mountain people, and we never considered or gave a thought to Texas. Don't get me wrong, we have great respect for the state; we just didn't see ourselves living there.

After a long, awkward silence, I mustered up all my maturity to say, "Are you freaking kidding me?" Again, silence. He eventually agreed he wasn't really sure about the area, but the job was what he was looking for, and he needed to get out of a bad job situation. His boss was toxic, and turnover was 400 percent. My husband was the last man standing, and he was paying the price for it emotionally, mentally, physically, and spiritually. Being the supportive, loving, and most amazing wife that I am, I agreed on one condition: We must have a pool!

With that, we began the process of moving. I solicited feedback from friends and associates who knew about the Houston area. Statements like, "It's the armpit of the state," "It's the butthole of the world," and "You couldn't pay me enough to live there" abounded. I heard stories of horrendous humidity and nasty bugs. I was told Houston had two seasons: hot and hell hot. I like the heat, but prefer a dry climate. And although mosquitoes love me, the feelings are not mutual!

We sold our Colorado house in one day. In fact, the Realtor didn't even have time to enter our MLS into the system. My husband gave his notice, so we were committed. Houston bound we were!

Houston, the Smiths Have Landed

The only time I had ever been to Houston was flying through on the way to a tropical destination. All I remember about the airport is it was hot and it smelled. Apparently, the air-conditioning was broken.

We had just a few days to explore the area and find a home. My introduction to the Houston area was a tour of the industrial and gas section of southeast Houston where, for as far as the eye could see, oil refineries dominated the landscape. Other than the overpasses, the city was flat as a pancake. I wanted to cry … until we started house hunting. I was quite impressed with the quality of homes and space between. We lived in California for ten years, where land is at a premium, meaning you don't got none! Colorado got the idea to follow California's lead, and homes are crammed in so close you can hear your neighbor snore. Our neighbors in Loveland, Colorado, were complete whackos. We kept expecting to see on the news how they had dead bodies stored in the basement; we were just glad we only had to deal with their verbal abuse.

Our Houston Realtor showed us some incredible communities, and we selected one on the very first day. Things were looking up!

That night, my husband broke a tooth eating dinner, and coming back to the hotel from the parking garage, he cracked his head on a low-hanging pipe. We spent the night in the emergency room. The next morning, I woke up sick. Were these signs telling us to "run; run very fast!" or were they obstacles to overcome? Didn't really matter since my husband started his job, and I was packing up our Colorado house. We'd moved before, and I knew the drill ... so I thought.

Houston, I Have a Problem!

I should have got a gun and told the movers to leave when one, whom we'll call Dewey, proved to have no IQ. No, I'm not exaggerating. For the three long days of the packing process, he could never get my name right: Lisa, Lora, Laurie, Linda, Lynn, and on and on. When you would tell him something stayed behind, he packed it up. When you explained something needed to go in a box, he threw it to the side. The driver was a real winner. He dropped so many F bombs I hardly knew what he was really saying, although I was bright enough to pick up on the fact he was complaining.

I'll save you the painstaking truth of a wretched pack job and sum up to say most everything we owned was damaged. They disassembled everything. Furniture we had for fourteen years arrived in pieces; they even deflated my exercise ball to save space. Really? Glass and fragile items were at the bottoms of boxes unwrapped, underneath, oh, say my blender and mixer! Picture frames were shattered, leather items scratched, upholstery ruined, and things missing—like the cord to the TV. Lucky me, I got to deal with these idiots for the unloading process, where the amazement continued; they dropped boxes, dumped items, and ruined the wood floor of our new house. I'm sorry, but all I could say was, "ARE YOU FREAKING KIDDING ME!??"

My hair fell out as I dealt with the aftermath of our move for months and months. Each and every repair man who came to fix something ended up creating more damage. At what point do you crawl in a hole and surrender? I don't know, because I am now a Texan, and I thought I'd better "cowboy up." I got us unpacked, settled in, and made our house a home.

For the Love of Houston!

Our home in Houston was everything we had hoped for (yes, I got a pool!), and we began meeting neighbors. Texans were proving to be might friendly folks. In fact, some of our neighbors took it upon themselves to set us straight. We were out working in the yard one day when a neighbor came over and said, "Don't you all know it is miserable out? Get inside!" Apparently, we looked as though we needed to go inside, but we chose to keep at it. Yes, we sweated, but hey, you reach a point where you can't possibly sweat anymore, right?

My husband, being the thoughtful man he is, used himself as the guinea pig. He sat on the grass in a park. "Wow, my butt is hot," he exclaimed. Then his hands were burning, covered in fire ants. Like Wesley from the movie, *The Princess Bride,* he learned "the secrets of the fire swamp, and we can now live there happily." What a guy!

We were indeed enjoying the warm weather, nice people, ocean access, and fresh fish. Then the mosquitoes arrived—with a vengeance! For about a two-week period, they attempted to take over the entire city of Houston. I was sitting in a restaurant bathroom being attacked, and shopping inside stores wasn't safe. Home Depot staff would come over and spray you with bug repellent! My mosquito bites had mosquito bites, and I just knew I was going to die for lack of blood! I mean, even the drive-through cleaners wasn't safe. Are you freaking kidding me?

Speaking of drive through, we have noticed Houstonians don't like to get out of their cars. I must say getting donuts on the go is pretty cool, um, so I'm told (pardon me, I need to wipe the powdery sugar off my fingers, as it's making my keyboard sticky). With stats of high rates of obesity, I wasn't expecting to see people running and biking in the hottest part of the day—repeatedly! We have discovered some awesome parks and love canoeing the bayous. I was a little uneasy about gliding right next to a gator, but he was a Texas gentleman and let us go by. I was definitely connecting with Houstonians. I ran outside, no matter what, every day. I hiked in 112 degrees and ran at altitudes of 10,000 feet and higher, but I'd never sweated so much in all my life as exercising in Houston. The upside? I don't have to wear umpteen layers or worry about frostbite, and that's fine with me. What I've decided about humidity is you don't have to shovel it!

Our dog loves the snow. He had quite the adjustment ... for like two seconds. The wildlife here is like being at doggy Disneyland every day. He's on sensory overload, and if he needs to cool off, he swims in the pool. His breed doesn't bark, and he only does so to warn us. I work from home, and one day he was barking his head off. *Oh great, someone is breaking in!* I thought, as I ran downstairs. He was focused and pointing at an enormous cockroach. Holy smokes! They weren't kidding when they said everything is bigger in Texas! I screamed like a girl, and the two of us went running to the other side of the house. Once again, I decided I'd better put my big-girl panties on, and I headed back to the scene of the crime, equipped with paper towels. As I approached the cockroach, the size of a VW bug, it flew at me—into my face. Are you freaking kidding me!? Suffice it to say the bug died and I lived, but it wasn't pretty. I called pest control, and they were out the next day.

Houstonians

After living in Houston for three years, I would like to say insanely large bugs didn't wig me out, but at least I knew what to expect. We put bug repellent in every room of the house *and* in our cars. Like the saying goes, "Don't leave home without it!"

I learned fences aren't for privacy but instead are passageways for squirrels. I discovered all the beautiful front doors might as well be bricked over. Texans come in the side door. I have come to the conclusion we really don't garden in Houston; we weed. Eesh, those things grow feet in a day!

I realized no one outside of Texas truly knows where Houston resides. "Is that near Dallas?" Really? We are only one of *the* healthiest cities in the union economically, who hardly had a recession and is kicking ass in the job and housing markets. And, I've concluded Texans must love Colorado, because without fail, when people find out we moved from Colorado to Houston, they say, "Are you freaking kidding me?" Well, the joke is on those who do not live here. They are missing out on some of the best weather (and yes, we have season— January is cold, damp, and rainy), friendliest people, beautiful birds, lakes, and waterways. They will never experience all the city has to offer, Texas sized. They are also paying a lot more for a much smaller house. Our cat loves this most of all, finding new places to snooze each day. He lets us live here with him, by the way.

I even figured out why Texans drive so daggum fast. They have to get their Blue Bell ice cream home before it melts! If you haven't ever tried Blue Bell, it really is amazing. I'm not even an ice cream fan, but the rich, natural ingredients truly set it apart.

I have come to appreciate the bumper sticker, "I wasn't born in Texas, but I got here as fast as I could!" Yes, despite a mountain of challenges and Texas-sized adjustments, we became Houstonians. We took walks and runs on the beach, meals at the Kemah Boardwalk, rode bikes on the Terry-Hershey path, and explored the Hill Country. Most of all, we fell in love with the people. We've were invited to more parties, barbeques, and community events than ever before. Folks welcomed us and said, "We're glad you've come!" To anyone considering a move to Houston, I would advise you to expect the worst, and you will be pleasantly surprised by the best! You definitely will want to keep a sense of humor, though.

What lies behind you and what lies in front of you,
pales in comparison to what lies inside of you.
~ RALPH WALDO EMERSON ~
Essayist

We Can Laugh, or We Can Cry

Life will always throw us curve balls. Just because I am now married to a wonderful man doesn't mean we won't have challenges and struggles. Trust me, we have had our fair share of both. Each of us has a choice, though. We can laugh or cry. We can focus on what we have or what we don't have; we can concentrate on what change takes away from us or see what it gives us. We can get bitter or better! I have chosen to trust God and believe with all my heart good comes of all frustrating, negative, and tough situations. Sometimes, this frame of mind is easier said than done.

Shortly after we married, I had a large consulting project monopolizing my time. The long-term contract and monthly retainer were enough to allow my husband to quit commercial fishing and start a business. I figured I would be the breadwinner long enough for him to get established, then we could live our dream together. Consequently, my husband quit his occupation of twenty years, and we bought a house near my client so I wouldn't have to travel. Within six months, my long-term contract was ended, even though they committed to five years in writing. Personally, I think I did too good of a job. I should have worked slower and not delivered everything so quickly. Besides, I think I scared the living crap out of all the men in the office who were very old school.

My husband and I were now both unemployed with a brand-new house payment. Just lovely! Yet I must say how relieved I was when God stepped in. He extracted me from a horrible situation. This client was truly dysfunctional with a lot of internal issues. I would have stuck it out until I ended up in the psychiatric ward, hospital, or six feet under, but God looked out for me once again by breaking this commitment for me.

Not knowing a soul in the area, we were force to lean upon each other, cleaving each other through the turbulence. I would like to say we handled everything like champions, but I will say this: we discovered a deep bond that forces of evil cannot break. We chose to embrace the area and made some wonderful memories. I have to say, though, I was glad to move on in four years to a richer chapter of our life.

Things Do Happen for a Reason

For years, we ran our own business and were experiencing great success, especially through international markets via our website. That is, until September 11, 2001. Everything changed. The phone stopped ringing, email ceased arriving in our inbox, and pending contracts dried up like raisins unpicked. We were faced yet again with financial woes and a house payment.

I had started a hobby in the fitness industry teaching classes, and I loved it. We lived in Southern California, where health and wellness were more important than gas in your car! I decided to get my certification in personal training and opened my own studio. Income immediately started coming in. Then one day, a client of mine asked me if I would help his company. He had some serious HR issues. I suggested my husband contact him, as he was the resident HR expert.

That led to a job offer, and my husband accepted. We decided one of us really needed the security of a steady paycheck. What felt like a devastating blow turned out to be an amazing door opened to a bright future for us both. My husband has enjoyed a fruitful career, and I continue to operate two businesses. Life is good.

When the stuff hits the fan, we can tend to feel punished or penalized. We feel singled out, but you must not submit to those lies for long. God is still in charge! He really does have a plan for us, and it is usually better than we ever expected. I have learned through the years God creates solutions so out of my sphere of understanding I must just trust and believe. Consider His ways a surprise gift. We don't know what is in the package, but we know we will just love it.

Bad things do happen; how I respond to them defines my character and the quality of my life. I can choose to sit in perpetual sadness, immobilized by the gravity of my loss, or I can choose to rise f rom the pain and treasure the most precious gift I have—life itself.
~ WALTER INGLIS ANDERSON ~
Painter

You Just Gotta Laugh

We did eventually make it to Phoenix, Arizona. Our dream came true! Let me tell you, though, even paradise has potholes. Soon after moving into our beautiful new home, the bathroom floor turned to dust. Yes, the tile just started to crumble apart. Oh joy! An expense we didn't expect. The tile floor was glued to the tub, and when they pulled the tub out, they learned it was permanently attached to the shower wall. Basically, our entire master bath had to be torn apart and rebuilt. We were promised two weeks, and five short months later, we had to fire the crew for doing the worst remodel job ever. The company made right by it, and we now enjoy a beautiful master bathroom designed the way we like.

Bliss did not last, and a few months later, when a pipe burst under the garage floor slab, a water geyser began gushing through the seams. All right, another expense! We immediately called our home warranty plan, but a plumber didn't come until the end of the following day. "Yup, you have a leak." With that, the plumber left. He said someone else would have to come out and find the specific location of the hole in the pipe. Another day went by, and a "leak locator" came. "Yup, you have a leak, and it is right here." They, too, left.

We waited and waited for days. Our assigned plumber did not return our calls or respond to our email. The home warranty/insurance folks said, "Sorry, it is out of our hands. You must work with your assigned plumber." After a week without running water, I was at my wit's end. I called a friend to have lunch and get out of the house and away from our drama for a moment. After our lovely Chinese lunch, I opened up my fortune cookie to read: "Come back later ... I am sleeping. Yes, cookies need their sleep, too."

You've got to be kidding me!?

Crying wouldn't change anything, so I let out a really big laugh. And with that, I let go. "This too shall pass," as does everything. Frustration will end, and tough times will turn to better days. All of this is a reminder for us, however. When things are going smoothly, let us rejoice and be grateful. Everything has a season, and all good things must come to an end. Let us not weep because they are over, but be glad that they happened! When life goes off the rails, get your sense of humor and lean upon the Lord.

More Tests

The last two years will go down in the record books for me. My husband lost his job, my mother in-law passed away, and I battled health issues once again. I will save you the long story this round, but I went two years misdiagnosed (again) before I finally got the help I needed. (Side note here: You have to be your own advocate!) I knew something was wrong, and no one would listen. I was told over and over again that I was just "old" and to quit complaining when my list of symptoms was a mile long. I had to stand my ground and fight to get to the bottom of my illness, which ended up being hypothyroid disease. It explained everything, and now that I know, I can defy my diagnosis!

Suffice it to say. I've had to reread my own material multiple times these last two years. If you should ever write a book, be forewarned that you *will* encounter everything you write about as an opportunity to ensure you really meant it. Ha! Yes, God has a sense of humor, and we must not lose ours ... *ever*. If you need to rest, rest. If you need a break, take one. However, don't ever lose hope or faith, because God has your back. Even when we can't see the change, He is working behind the scenes.

Believe

Throughout this recent struggle, Lauren Daigle's song "You Say" has made me cry yet lifted my spirits at the same time. I'll leave you with the chorus lyrics:

> *You say I am loved when I can't feel a thing*
> *You say I am strong when I think I am weak*
> *You say I am held when I am falling short*
> *When I don't belong, oh You say that I am Yours*
> *And I believe (I), oh I believe (I)*
> *What You say of me (I)*
> *I believe*

DEFY YOUR DIAGNOSIS CHAPTER ELEVEN

FIT Life Formula @ Work

Write about a time when you wanted to cry but just had to laugh.

Looking back at a difficult time in your life, what lessons did you learn?

What helps you keep your sense of humor?

CHAPTER TWELVE

Never Give Up!

Never give up, for that is just the place and time that the tide will turn.
~ HARRIET BEECHER STOWE ~
Author

When asked what the mantra of my life is, my reply is, "Never give up!" I came from a low-income, single-parent family household before such a thing existed. As you know by now, my father died of cancer when I was the tender age of thirteen, leaving me and my mom to "press on." I learned at a very young age things didn't come easy. We had to pull ourselves together and continue to live life, even when we didn't feel like it. This traumatic event in my life launched me on a path of self-discovery and personal challenge that continues to drive me toward maximum success in all areas of life.

When You Have the Will, a Way Will Come

I began charting my course then, and prepared to pay my own way through college. Working over fifty hours a week, I attended night school to obtain my associate's degree in OIT and then on to my bachelor's degree in Business Marketing and Communications. By my midtwenties, I was the youngest employee to achieve director status at a publishing company in Colorado Springs, running the four-plus-million-dollar business. All the while, I had a passion for fitness. An energetic individual, I enjoyed pushing myself with outdoor activities such as hiking, biking, skiing, and playing sports like tennis and volleyball. If I hadn't tried it before, I would attempt to master it and usually would in a short amount of time.

Not until 1996, however, when my mother was diagnosed with a terminal brain tumor and I left my abusive husband did I realize my life wasn't balanced. I spent so much energy on climbing the corporate ladder I forgot to care for my total being. My self-esteem was shattered, and weighing in at just 97 pounds, I wanted to give up. I had to make a difficult decision: Take the easy route and just fade away or make some drastic changes in my life. I wasn't raised to quit, so I opted to improve the quality of my life.

A Big Step

I embarked on a healing journey, learning I needed to do more than just care for my physical condition with exercise. I also needed to attend to my emotional, mental, and spiritual health as well. Upon my mother's death in May of 1997, I decided to take a huge step of faith and moved to Washington State, where I started my own consulting business, helping businesses across the country grow and succeed. Within a year, I had remarried, and my business was thriving. Still, I had always dreamed of being a fitness instructor, so when I moved to California with my new husband, whom I met in Washington, I took trainings and began obtaining all the credentials I could to help others get "totally" fit. Steve provided such a safe and loving environment I was able to come into myself for the first time in my life. He gave me the courage to soar! I am now an AFAA Certified Fitness Instructor, Kickboxing Instructor, and Advanced Personal Trainer as well as an Indoor Cycling® Instructor and Advanced Certified Human Behavior Consultant.

My business expanded to not only offer consulting services but also corporate trainings and life coaching. I found myself helping more and more people find balance in their lives. I was able to use my corporate experience and valuable life lessons for the benefits of others. The process took four years, but I finally reached more people with encouragement, hope, and ways to manage their life better with my first book, *A Healthier, Happier You!* Once again, I did not give up! This little book helps readers understand the negative impact of stress (illness, strained relationships, disease, overeating, undereating, drugs, and alcohol abuse) and then provides practical yet powerful ways to cancel chaos and replace it with balance. It is light, inspirational, and easy to read, but don't let its size fool you. Even though it is compact, it is chock-full of ideas that will literally change your life for the better. You can purchase it on my website: www.lorrainebosse-smith.com/store/stressmanagement/.

Keep Keeping On

I haven't stopped. I built up my own private fitness studio to work with clients one on one and helped countless people get healthy. I have written seven additional books and produced three fitness videos, all available on my website, of course. Although I have since closed my personal training studio, I continue to teach dynamic, energetic fitness classes when I can. I offer keynote speeches to larger groups and provide executive recruiting with the intent to transform lives with my FIT Leadership Formula. I have found success where others have failed. My mantra of, "Never give up" has paid off. I am healthy and strong. I've overcome relationship challenges, health issues, and just about every business roadblock. I am still active hiking and playing tennis. Unlike earlier years, I enjoy balance and peace through caring for my total self. I continue to coach individuals, helping them achieve their personal and professional goals, and I speak and train across the country. All this to say, NEVER give up!

Have Faith

When I moved to Seattle, Washington, I was nervous. I mean, I hate the rain and gray clouds. Colorado is second only to California in sunny days, which is what I grew up with. Besides, I only had $500 to my name. My ex kept a lot of my stuff, and I was basically starting over at the age of thirty. I only knew two friends from high school, one of which who offered his couch to me. I didn't even have a blanket! I slept covered up by my jacket. I had worked so hard getting myself high up the ladder, only to fall hard.

I didn't have much to start a business, but I had faith. I believed with all my heart, soul, and mind God led me to this point in my life. Within days, I had several clients, one being quite lucrative. I was making more money than with my job! I learned to put my trust in God, not in man. Although a job offers some sense of security, our only true security is in Him.

I thought my life was beyond repair, but God showed me otherwise. Everything I lost was restored and then some. If you are feeling lost and discouraged, have faith. God knows where you are, and He has plans for you. We just have to understand His plans may be different than what we originally thought.

"For my thoughts are not your thoughts,
neither are your ways my ways," declares the LORD.
~ Isaiah 55:8 ~

Do the Work

Relationships do take work, but they can be so worth it. We were designed for connection, but we can sometimes forget relationships can be inconvenient and messy. We aren't robots! We have feelings, moods, thoughts, fears, anxieties, hopes, and the ability to love beyond ourselves. When we tap into that, we can have the richest experience on the planet. We can also turn a blind eye and live a nightmare.

A commercial for a cable company plays out a father's decision not to buy cable, which leads to his daughter hanging out with questionable characters. This, in turn, leads her to marrying a jerk and having a weird baby. Each decision we make does have consequences. Relationships are no different. We often give more consideration to what we will eat for dinner than we do to the people we will hang out with, date, or let into our "inner circle."

Right now, you probably feel like the relationships you do have require too much time … how could you possibly give more? Yet at the same time, you may feel isolated. It is not uncommon for us to feel like we are being tugged on by a million people, but we still don't feel connected to any single one. Quality. You see, when we let *quantity* get out of control, we become spread too thin. No one single relationship is able to fully develop *quality*-wise.

If you want to soar with the eagles, then you need to say NO to the turkeys! How? You need to know what matters to you. Let's look at your relationships for a minute. How do you get along with your spouse/mate? How about your children? What about your parents, siblings, extended family, in-laws? Then we have our friends, co-workers, church members, etc. Somewhere in that list is a person that you are not getting along with, and it is sucking the life right out of you.

My mother told me when I was young that my siblings were family by blood, but it didn't mean we would automatically be best friends. She wisely advised me not to put that kind of pressure on the relationship. If I did, I'd probably be disappointed. Television shows like *The Waltons* portray "the perfect family," but it rarely exists. We can spend a lifetime trying to make our family fit the television mold, but we will just end up frustrated and worn-out. What we need to learn is manage our expectations and put our energy into the right relationships.

If you expect perfection from other people,
your whole life is a series of disappointments,
grumbling, and complaints. If, on the contrary,
you pitch your expectations low, taking
folks as the inefficient creatures which they are,
you are frequently surprised by having them
perform better than you had hoped.
~ BRUCE BARTON ~
Politician & author

Know Thyself

Managing our expectations requires us to look inward first. For those who are single, let me say this: better to be single than to be married to the wrong person! Being single may be lonely, but being miserable is painful and stressful. I have known too many women who married because they desperately wanted children, so they "settled." Everyone loses, especially the children, who didn't ask for the hardship. In order to prevent marrying "Mr. Wrong," you must first know yourself. What are you looking for in a mate? For those who have already walked down the aisle, having a clear picture of what matters to you can help your existing relationship. In some cases, you may realize why you have tension. If you married a non-Christian, but that was high on your priority list, you can't expect him to change. You can hope and pray, but you married him as he was, and accepting this will reduce your conflict. Instead, look at the areas that you match up well and build upon those.

Eharmony.com and other dating services are brilliant. They understand the premise of matching up our values with another person to increase our chances of success. What are your top ten qualities that you won't budge on as a single? What matters most to you being married?

What values do you hold in esteem with your family and friends? List them out here. Some things on your list might be: a Christian, athletic, smart, outgoing, faithful, honest, funny, trustworthy, etc.

MY TOP TEN LIST

_____   _____

_____   _____

_____   _____

_____   _____

_____   _____

I heard someone say once that disappointment is our expectations not met. That hit me between the eyes. Too often, we blame others for our disappointments when the reality is that we didn't get what we wanted. Ouch.

This made me reflect on arguments I've had with my husband. How many times was I mad simply because I didn't get it my way? Frank Sinatra may have done it "my way," but in a real world, we must compromise. If we value the relationship, we must put it first over our own needs some times. Therefore, managing our expectations also necessitates us to take a look in the mirror. We are the common denominator in all our relationships. No matter where we run, we keep showing up! Ever move away when you hit the bottom, hoping that your new location would be better. Guess what, when we do this, we bring our own issues, desires, and demands with us. Be careful that you aren't imposing them on others.

At the heart of personality is the need to feel a senseof being lovable,
without having to qualify for that acceptance.
~ Maurice Wagner ~
Christian counselor

Take Inventory

Start evaluating your relationships to determine if you have been expecting too much. People can only be who they are and do what they know. Turtles don't fly! If you continually put pressure on a turtle to soar like an eagle, all you will get is irritated. The turtle will finally retreat into his shell in disgust. Ladies, we can be guilty of expecting our men to be more life us. God didn't want us to be exactly the same. We are supposed to be like a hand and glove, fitting together. Try accepting "the turtle" as is and learn to appreciate him for what he brings to the relationship. When we give unconditional love like this, often people will try harder to improve. They will feel more loved, and you won't have near the stress. Everyone wins!

Turtles can't fly!

Take Inventory

Besides expecting people to be what we want them to be, we can also put our energy into the wrong people. This is a tough one, because we want to love all and be good to all. This is an admirable goal, but even Jesus couldn't minister in His own village. We have to admit our humanness and limitations. Men have their egos when it comes to career, sports, and macho stuff. I believe we have it when it comes to relationships—we believe we can do it all! Well, if you are overweight, stressed, tired, or sick, your body is telling you that you can't. Accept it. This doesn't mean you are a failure; you are simply human.

I've been working on this very thing, and you know what? It is actually a relief to know I'm not perfect. Oh, I knew that in my head my entire life, but to literally stop *trying* was freeing. So, who are you giving too much of yourself to? I want you to take some inventory here. We looked at some possessions early on and how we need to detach a bit so that we put "things" in their place. We need to put some relationships in their place as well. Under each heading, write out your relationships and how much time you spend (high or low), then rate them yes or no for energizing and draining:

Immediate Family Member	Time Spent	Energizes Me	Drains Me

Extended Family Member	Time Spent	Energizes Me	Drains Me

Friend's Name	Time Spent	Energizes Me	Drains Me

Co-Worker's Name	Time Spent	Energizes Me	Drains Me

Church Member's Name	Time Spent	Energizes Me	Drains Me

Other Name	Time Spent	Energizes Me	Drains Me

The clearer you are about these things, the less likely you will be to attach yourself to the wrong people, like I have in the past. Be an active participant in your own life! Weigh out the pros and cons of any relationship and determine if it is right for you. The truth is, we only have so much energy in any given day. Where and with whom do you want to spend it? Do you want to feel uplifted, recharged, and full of life or drained as a result? The choice is yours.

The best way to attract eagles is to be one. You will never regret working on yourself.

Seek Wisdom

One important investment to make is in wisdom. We all lack it in some areas, and we all have it to share in others, depending on our unique circumstances and situations. That's why I'm a firm believer in mentoring. I've been blessed to have some incredible examples of stellar leaders in my life, but I have also witnessed examples of very poor managers. In either case, I was able to build my own leadership style based on what I saw. But seeing isn't always enough. We must learn.

A mentor is a trusted confidant, a coach or guide, and we all need one. A mentor is someone who walks besides you, encouraging you along the way. Mentors provide invaluable input and feedback, not always telling you what you *want* to hear but what you *need* to hear—always with your best interest at heart. They impart their wisdom into our lives. What an incredible gift!

I've had mentors since the age of seventeen. I would seek out an individual I admired: professional, aggressive, kind, stable, strong, confident, capable, and talented. I would ask them to invest in my life. I've never been turned down. In fact, most people are honored by the request. Over the years, my mentors have been bosses, peers, and even competitors whom I was close to personally. In all cases, these people allowed me to ask critical questions regarding not only my career but my personal life. These people have helped steer me through some rough waters, and with their support, I have continued to grow, mature, and blossom.

My mentors have been both men and women, although I do recommend at least one same-sex mentor. Why? I was recently asked this question, and here was my reply: Women have unique challenges and circumstances to which they face in the world. A woman mentor will relate much better. Conversely, men have their own pressures and stress, often tied with being the sole provider for their family. The bottom line is ensuring your mentor understands firsthand your situation.

Do make sure you feel comfortable with your mentor and trust him or her. For the relationship to work, you must know without a doubt the information shared will remain confidential. I usually prefer someone older than me because I gain so much life experience and wisdom, but peers certainly can contribute. Look for someone in your field or an area you desire to move toward. I suggest you meet with your mentor monthly if both your schedules permit. Grab lunch together or arrange a telephone call if your mentor is long distance. Value their time by coming prepared with specific questions or concerns. Their job is to keep you on track and assist you with mapping out your future. Be honest and open with them.

If you are struggling to find a mentor, you can always hire a professional coach. I assist people with their career goals, life issues, health, stress, and a myriad of other things. Although I do not believe coaches need to have a specific degree or certification to coach, they must have the experience you seek. They should also be walking their talk. If you hire someone to make you a millionaire, and they are driving around in a beat-up used car, keep looking. You can learn more about what coaching is and isn't at my website (www.lorrainebosse-smith.com) under Coaching.

A mentor is an adviser, counselor, and a teacher. We can all be one. You may not feel like you have much to offer, but someone is always in need of the valuable knowledge you have learned. Life is all about sharing and giving back what others have given to you by seeking out someone in need of guidance. Mentoring is even mentioned in the Bible with the Peter, Barnabus, and Timothy principle. We are all three, sometimes at the same time, other times at different stages of our life. I thoroughly enjoy this aspect of my business. I find great fulfillment and satisfaction in helping others aim for excellence! Perhaps a co-worker or younger friend would benefit tremendously from a mentor. Be committed and faithful to this person. You won't regret the investment in the life of another. We are all striving to be our best, and mentoring is a sure way of helping us each be all God intended us to be.

Do Your Best on the Path You Are On

God calls each of us to be something different, and sometimes, what we are to be isn't what we thought. In the movie *War Horse*, a thoroughbred horse is bought by a poor family to farm their land. Joey, the name given to him by Albert, the main character, is designed by God to race, but never does. Instead, he plows hard, rocky ground. Then World War I strikes, and he is bought by the military, against Albert's wishes. Unfortunately, his dad has a drinking problem, and they will lose the farm without the money. Joey goes to war and sees things not fit for man or beast. His lieutenant is killed in battle, and the Germans seize him. He escapes for a while and lives with a sweet little girl who is ill. He becomes her entire world until he's captured again by the Germans. This time, Joey is forced to haul heavy artillery up steep hills. On the brink of death, he gets away. Ultimately, he is reunited with his owner, who ended up getting wounded in a trench.

At a glance, this story seems bleak and depressing. Joey was designed for better. You need only look at him to see he was made for speed. He could have been a contender! He should have been treated like a superstar racehorse heading toward the finish line instead of running away from danger. Alas, life had other plans. If you look closer and deeper, however, this horse was given incredible opportunities to touch lives he would have never known from a race track.

Joey bonded deeply with a young boy. Training a horse took discipline, and saying goodbye to his beloved horse took courage. Both molded Albert, and he became a good man. Joey also helped the boy's poor family keep their farm, and he assisted a lieutenant die honorably with valor. Joey saved countless lives of people on the battle field by pulling them to safety. Joey then gave a sick little girl hope and joy for the few days on earth she had. He encouraged a fellow horse to fight the good fight, inspiring the humans who took note. Joey brought enemies together if even for just a moment, and he loved a boy with all he had.

Each one of these is powerful, but Joey does them all. Was this the life he thought he would have? No. He became a war horse, not a race horse. But he gave his best to what life brought him. Isn't that all any of us can do?

ↂ

Positive thinking is important, but we must know and realize that, despite all our desires, life may throw us onto another path. Be and do the best you can on that path. Give and love people you meet along the way, and you may realize you did indeed get to run and run fast—it just wasn't on a race track. We may not get medals or ribbons, but if we respect and honor ourselves and others, we *will* have won, God willing.

Different Paths

One of the paths some seem to be called on is the SWAMP. These SWAMP people are **S**piritual **W**alkers **A**mong **P**eople. They haven't crossed completely over to the safe security of the shore, and they may never. Others have been blessed to reach the safety of the shore and can clean up and celebrate their journey. They give hope to those of us in the swamp crossing our murky obstacles *is* possible, and we may eventually come out the other side victoriously. The shore people are waiting with fresh water and food, arms wide open to embrace those who step upon the shore.

For those in the swamp, though, we are the experts. We know the secrets of the swamp because we have been in it a while. We have learned how to not only cope but adapt. Our role is to help *others* get through the swamp alive, and although we could get to the shore, we remain. I used to think I had a mountain to climb and would reach the summit someday to experience incredible views. I now realize I am called to stay in the yucky swamp, because many people get stuck. Without help, they will be consumed and drown. Alligators and venomous snakes lurk and await their lethal attack. SWAMP walkers not only guide people through, but they protect them.

Like Joey, I often think I was made to do something grander and certainly more glamorous. However, knowing I have rescued, saved, and assisted hurting people traverse some bleak conditions is rewarding. I have to accept I will forever be muddy.

We each are called to different roles and must our own paths. All are needed. Not one position is more important than the other. If you find yourself in the swamp, don't give up! Our suffering has a purpose, sometimes not just for our own life but that of others.

Defy the Odds

I am not a football fan whatsoever, but I do admire and respect Peyton Manning for coming back after his injuries. He was most likely told to quit football, but he chose to overcome his obstacles. He's proof we must fight for our health. He didn't listen to the naysayers who claimed he was washed up. He focused on getting stronger and better, and his first year with the Denver Broncos proved everyone wrong. He was still a champion!

I was told in my twenties I'd never be able to do anything high impact every again, yet I teach fitness classes. In my thirties, I was told I had a disease without a cure, but I beat it and won. In my forties, I was told I would be in pain for the rest of my life and would never run again. Not only am I pain-free, but I run every day and completed a marathon. Don't be the kind of person who uses bad news from a doctor to give up on the things you love. If you have, decide today to get your life back. If I had listened to the doctors, I'd be addicted to pain meds and wheelchair bound. Instead, I enjoy my active life, and you can, too!

Expect Obstacles

I've been a personal trainer long enough to know for a fact as soon as a person finally decides to put their health first, they encounter resistance from the universe. Literally, their lives begin to unravel before their very eyes: car accidents, falls, family illness, job issues, sickness, injuries, and marriage problems—you name it, and it hits folks square between the eyes.

I've decided to believe the universe is actually doing them a favor, because when the obstacles come, it forces people to decide how serious they really are about getting healthy. I mean when things crumble in your hand, you have to be very determined to stay the course. As their personal trainer, I cheer them on to fight the good fight, stay with it, and overcome their adversities. Although I can help them be motivated, the reality is, all of them must decide for him or herself they WILL improve their health.

Regardless of your goals, aspirations, or journey, expect obstacles. Embrace the potholes as they come and laugh in the face of frustration, telling the universe, *Ha! Is that all you've got?* Let nothing, and I mean nothing, stand in YOUR way of becoming a better you. This is your life!

Planes, Trains, and Terrorists

Some obstacles are bigger than others. September 11, 2001, is a day that will never be forgotten. It's the type of event you remember exactly where you were and what you were doing at the time the tragedy struck our country. I was in Minneapolis on a business trip. I flew in on Monday night from California. I actually had a great flight out, which was unusual as I normally experienced four or more hours delay going through San Francisco. I arrived to my destination right on time.

Monday ended up being the calm before the storm, as on Tuesday morning when I awoke, I witnessed the airplane crashing into the second tower of the World Trade Center, right before my very eyes, live on television. As events unfolded and I watched yet another plane dive into the Pentagon, I began to grasp what was happening: America was under attack.

My first call was to my husband, who wasn't awake yet back in California. Attempting to shut the alarm off (actually the phone ringing), he didn't pick up. I left a message regarding the severe situation. My second call was to the car rental agency: "I am keeping my car. I don't know where or when I'm dropping it off." My heart hoped I would be able to fly out, but my logic knew otherwise. All flights had been canceled, and all airports were closed for the first time in our history. I was alone in Minneapolis.

I went to have breakfast, although I couldn't eat much. The restaurant was packed with people talking about the morning's events. Strangers gathered to watch a small television that had been put up. I didn't feel alone any longer; our country was uniting together.

I did have a decision to make: Did I stay at the hotel and attempt to get home, or did I continue on with my business trip? My emotions were beginning to unsettle as I felt a burning desire to just get home. I felt like Dorothy in *The Wizard of Oz*: "There is no place like home!" I also had a responsibility to my client who paid for my trip to conduct business for them. I was at a crossroads. *Should I stay or should I go?*

I chose to proceed to my appointment in Minneapolis. Minimally, I needed to keep this meeting. I have to admit, though, my heart wasn't in it. My mind raced with images of an exploding plane, a burning building, and the knowledge of the many victims trapped inside. My spirit was ticked off, truth be told. I was angry at the people who did this, and I didn't want them to win by me cowering and giving up. So I pressed on.

My husband reached me shortly after my appointment, and I explained my dilemma. My next stop would have been Grand Rapids, Michigan, which is approximately 750 miles away. He encouraged me to lay low and wait it out in Minneapolis. He wanted me to be safe. Just then, something exploded on the highway. I didn't see it, but I was stuck along with hundreds of others on the freeway, the only road out of town. What may seem a "sign" to turn back and stay put to some motivated me even more to continue on. I would not live in fear. I would not back down and allow these evil people to win! I decided to drive cross-country. I compromised with my husband and assured him I would stop for a few hours to rest. We would stay in close contact via cell phone along the way.

The explosion was not an act of terrorism as originally noted on the radio. A truck crashed containing propane. Regardless, traffic didn't move for three hours. I felt helpless, and I could only imagine how the families of the victims felt. My heart was heavy, and my mind foggy. The drive ahead was long, and my only company was the radio with word of the devastation in New York City and the Pentagon flooding my ears. The buildings collapsed, taking with it the hope of survivors.

All in all, I drove 1,500 miles to each destination I needed to reach. I ended up in Cincinnati, Ohio, where hardly a road wasn't being worked on and every gas station was a complete zoo. It was Thursday now, and I was ready to go home. I *needed* to go home. I canceled the last leg of my trip to Virginia Beach, as I didn't want to go that far east, and I was out of gas.

I arrived at the airport at 5:30 a.m. to return my car. I waited in line one and half hours, along with four hundred people behind me. My flight was canceled, rebooked, canceled, and rebooked again. My bag was searched completely, every dirty sock. As I looked around, I noticed not one person was impatient or rude. Americans were showing their spirit and strength.

I was apprehensive to fly, but I knew I must—not just to get home but also to prove we will not be defeated. We were on the runway when the pilot softly said, "We have a light out. We'll need maintenance." That was the last word we heard for over an hour. We sat far from the terminal on the runway, and all flights had stopped departing. We were isolated away from the main terminal. One by one, the airline personnel on the flight with us were being called to the back of the plane. Something was happening, and we all knew it. Some women started crying. I called my husband to tell him I loved him and how he meant everything to me. I had heard so many "last cell phone calls" my heart was in my throat. I was scared for my life, but I knew I had to be brave. If our plane exploded, at least we wouldn't take anyone else out.

We had four suspects, one who was confirmed on the FBI "watch list" for terrorists. The police squad came out and apparently cleared us to come back to the terminal, where authorities immediately boarded to escort the four Middle Easterners away. We were told to deplane as quickly as possible—"Run, don't walk!" I hung up with my husband, as I noticed we were surrounded by emergency vehicles. Once we were off the plane, the K-9 crew and bomb squad searched the plane with a fine-tooth comb.

After several delays in the flight, we reboarded the flight and headed to Los Angeles. I never prayed so much in my life. I thanked God for each and every family member and friend. I relived experiences and blessings. Somehow, nothing really mattered and everything mattered. I didn't care if my bag made it. I didn't care about long lines or inconveniences. I just wanted to get home. I wanted to be with people. I wanted to celebrate life—the little things. Throughout the long flight, not a word was spoken among the passengers. Yes, I believe we were all praying that day.

When the pilot informed us we would be landing shortly, many sobbed, men and women alike. I held myself together. My husband greeted me at our small-town airport—which never looked so good—with a warm and loving embrace. At that point, I had nothing left and released all emotion. We didn't let go for a long time.

I made a decision to press on during a turbulent time in our country, but every day, we are each faced with tough situations, disappointments, conflict, illness, broken relationships, and a myriad of other negative things we must deliberately choose to push past. We can either sit down or we can be brave. Courage isn't a lack of fear but rather proceeding ahead despite it.

Courage isn't a lack of fear
but rather proceeding ahead despite it.

I don't know what exactly you are facing, but I do know you are braver than you think. God's spirit lives within us, giving us strength beyond understanding.

Be Grateful

Even if your life has had challenges, it is your life, and God gave it to you. What an awesome gift! Thank Him for it. Do you have a roof over your head? Do you have food to eat? Clothes to wear? Be thankful because some do not have even these basics. Extend appreciation for the people in your life and their health. Too often, we take for granted our blessings. In fact, make a list of everyone you are thankful for right now:

I AM THANKFUL FOR . . .

_____   _____

_____   _____

_____   _____

_____   _____

_____   _____

In times of difficulty, always ask, *What is good about this?* God doesn't point His almighty finger at us to "make us pay," but He does promise that good things *will* come out of our adversity.

I've just spent the last three years in treatment for Lyme disease, which is on top of the six years of my life going undiagnosed with bizarre symptoms and pain. I've had some dark days, but God's strength pulled me through. And, He has given me some amazing gifts as a result: compassion, understanding, support, love and the ability to extend grace to myself. I've always been one to raise the bar high for myself. Sure, I can encourage others to be easy on themselves, but I had to really practice that on myself this last year. I learned it was okay to rest and ask for help!

What has God given you this past year? Take a minute to write out a few of your hurdles and the blessings that resulted from them:

CHALLENGE	BLESSING

If you are in the midst of a tough time, you may not be able to see the blessing yet, and that is totally okay. Trust God for it even though you don't know what it looks like just yet. It will come.

Let Go and Let God

Now thank God again for all He has given you. When we focus on the good and turn over the bad to God, we have more energy to move ahead. I don't know about you, but my load gets awful heavy some times. Let God carry it. Taking on too much between work and home? Let go of some things! Refer back to the Circle of Influence and remind yourself that you can only really change yourself. Work on that and your relationship with God, and you will see greater results … like inner peace, improved health, and renewed energy. So with that, list out what is keeping you awake at night (work and home). What are you worrying about? Then reflect on whether or not you can change it. If you can, list the action required (talk to someone, get help, etc.) If not, write in the words, *Turn it over to God!*

ISSUE	CAN I CHANGE?	ACTION REQUIRED	LET GOD!

Trust God

Over lunch recently, I was talking with some friends on how it can be easier to turn things over to God but harder to let Him keep them. How true! We think we understand it more thoroughly and can do it better. Or we panic and think God may not have time for it. We are so wrong. Just as we delegate assignments at work, we must not only give God our issue but the authority to do something about it. Otherwise, we are tying His hands behind His back. Have you ever been in a position where you were given the task but not the authority to get it done? It is frustrating and counterproductive. We want less stress and more balance, right? Well, when we give something to God, let Him keep it. Save your energy for something else!

Perspective

I'm a movie fan, and I recently watched the HBO miniseries *The Pacific* again. Trust me, after seeing what our soldiers endured, your problems won't seem so bad. They rose to the occasion, fought endless battles, and survived on very little. Because of them, the war was won. Whatever battle you are facing, you must fight it. You must be 100 percent in it and committed to it. You have but one life. Make it count. If you botched things up, fix them. If your entire life has derailed, get back on track. If your life has been broken into a million pieces, pick up what counts, and get going. Small steps get us there, but never, EVER give up.

DEFY YOUR DIAGNOSIS CHAPTER TWELVE

FIT Life Formula @ Work

Look back at your list of challenges. Which one is the most difficult for you and why?

Have you truly turned this over to God, or have you taken it back?

Could you possibly be a SWAMP walker, called to help others? Pray about this and see what God tells you.

Name one person who energizes you and commit to getting together with them within the week!

CHAPTER THIRTEEN

Do Things Your Way

Very little is needed to make a happy life;
it is all within yourself, in your way of thinking.
~ MARCUS AURELIUS ~
Roman emperor

I spent my youth hating my flat chest. To say I was an A bra size is being generous. I literally had two different body types stuck together: Olive Oyl on the top, and Popeye on the bottom. My lower body has always been curvy and strong, but my top was like a diving board. Oh, how I dreaded the locker room! All the girls in junior high seemed to have developed breasts, and I kept waiting … and waiting well past high school. I could trim down my legs, but no amount of exercise would increase my breast size—trust me, I tried them all! "We must, we must, we must increase our bust!" is a bunch of bull, and so is any cream claiming to grow bigger breasts.

Through the years, I decided boobs really didn't matter—to those who *have* them. I can't speak for all flat-chested or small-breasted women, but I know I felt defective. I used to believe I was taken off the assembly line before I was complete. God's announcer said, "Boobs here!" and I must have heard, "Tubes here!" so I slid down one. Wheeeee! Away I went, breastless! I looked like a man with a butt. I often asked God, "What happened? Why am I not normal?" All I could see were all the women who had healthy-sized breasts. I was always comparing myself to others. I didn't see what I had that they didn't; all I could see was their boobs.

Bless my mom's heart; she tried to console me. During my teens, she offered to have my boobs done. I was utterly insulted. This just made me feel worse. "Great, so my own mother thinks I am inadequate?" I know this wasn't her intent, but I wasn't ready. Looking back, I am very glad I waited.

My Acceptance

As a personal trainer, I help people transform their bodies. Unfortunately, no amount of exercise will change certain features, like breasts. In my opinion, plastic surgery can help the outside of one's body, but it never can fix what is on the inside. Until we deal with our issues, no amount of plastic surgery will make us feel better. I spent years wrestling with my body's flaws. Aligning myself with abusive men who told me I was fat and flat didn't help. I know now I was only attracted to low-life men because I believed I deserved to be treated like garbage. My self-image was in the basement.

After an awful divorce from a truly wicked man, combined with my mother's death that same year, I was forced to tackle the tough stuff. Through my healing process, I learned to love myself as God made me. I appreciated how my strong my legs were; they allowed me to hike many mountains and run races. I was glad my arms weren't bulky but were sleek and defined. And finally, I could accept my small breasts were an asset for the active lifestyle I led. I mean, who wants to be smashed in the face by their boobs when running or jumping and get black eyes? I'd seen the contraptions large-breasted women had to wear to exercise—no thanks!

I was truly at peace with myself for the first time in my life. I wore shorter skirts, tighter jeans, and fitted shirts. I was okay with who I was, whose I was (God's), and what I looked like. I was then blessed richly and married a wonderful man. I joked and said, "Well, I certainly know he isn't marrying me for my money or my boobs, because I have neither!" I lost most everything in my divorce and was in the process of rebuilding my life. I never imagined finding my soul mate so quickly, but I did. God is good!

My Decision

Steve and I had been married four years when we moved to Southern California, the land of the beautiful. I would not have been able to live in California with my low self-esteem, but I fit right in as a health-oriented individual. I loved living in California and didn't struggle one bit with my image.

One day, I saw an ad for breast augmentation. I must have stared at the ad for hours. I was taken aback how I was actually considering it. I thought I was past that—and I was. The truth is, I didn't get the boob job to feel better or look sexier. I didn't do this for my husband, obviously. He didn't care; he loved me for me. The reality is, I got sick and tired of not fitting in clothes. I was two different sizes: extra small on top, and medium on the bottom. I couldn't get business suits or bikinis unless I could buy the pieces separately. And let's face it, some clothing, like bras, look better when you actually have something to put in it. I told my husband what I was planning to do, and he supported me either way.

I met with the doctor, who was as French as they come. He had absolutely no bedside manner, but he was a perfectionist—exactly what I wanted in a surgeon. I must have told him a hundred times I didn't want to go big. Even on the table just before I was knocked out, I grabbed his arm and reminded him, "Do not make them too big!" He laughed. Most women don't regret having the surgery, but wish they had gone bigger. Not me. I am thrilled with my C cup. It fits my frame, and, apparently, they look natural, because no one said anything. Only a select few of my friends knew about my breast augmentation surgery in December of 2002—not because I was embarrassed, but because I really thought they'd notice. I assumed I would tell everyone when they asked about it. I mean, you can't hide the fact you went from AA to C, especially the first couple of weeks, when your boobs are up under your chin!

My Surprise

I had visions of my friends and family saying, "Oh my God! You have boobs!" I pictured how I would smile big and reply, "Yes, I do! Do you like them?" No such conversations ever happened, and frankly, I was disappointed. Not even in the locker room at the gym did anyone say, "My, your breasts are perky for your age." Again, I dreamed of standing up nice and tall, saying, "Aren't they great?" I suspect breasts are somewhat personal, and perhaps people didn't want to offend me. Plastic surgery has come a long way, but some still consider it controversial. I stand by my original opinion: Surgery can't make you feel better about yourself. I think we see addictions to cosmetic improvements because the people have never dealt with their hurts, wounds, and issues. I did. I was planning on living with my body as it was, but then I decided to do something that would make life easier *for* me. After my surgery, I joined the ranks of many women, They are just boobs! I felt free.

Years have passed, and I have had the twins, as my husband calls them, for about fifteen years. Slowly, I share about my surgery when the topic comes up. Every doctor, massage therapist, or healthcare provider knows. I just have never felt inclined to walk up to people and tell them, "Hey, I have fake boobs!" In California, most women do, so no one would really care. If I made a big deal about it, they would just think, *She must be off her meds!* Ha! But I know, and I am grateful I can buy clothes that fit now. I don't have to fixate on what I don't have; I am whole … inside and out.

> *God has given us two incredible things:*
> *Awesome ability and freedom of choice.*
> *The tragedy is that, for the most part,*
> *many of us have refused both.*
> ~ FRANK DONNELLY ~
> *Baseball player*

Listen to Your Heart

This decision was mine and mine alone. Some people will shout out a "good for you!" In fact, I met a lady at the breast diagnostic center recently who offered immediately how she had fake boobs. We both had abnormal mammograms and were in for the next steps. Within a few minutes, she shared how her "girls" were over twenty years old and holding up nicely. I, of course, told her about mine. We shared a laugh and moved forward. Never in a million years would I have thought I could be so carefree about a subject that used to be so touchy.

I am very aware others may frown upon what I did. They will cast their judgment upon me, saying I didn't have enough faith or truly love what God gave me. Either way, I don't care. I had to do right by me, and I have spent too much of my life worrying about what others think. No more! I've also tried to please other people, like many, and the older I get, I realize first and foremost, we must make ourselves happy. If we run around taking care of everyone else but not ourselves, we become martyrs. We will be more and be able to give more when we ourselves are happy.

We must stop trying to please everyone, especially when it is at the expense of our own happiness. Quiet all the voices and listen to your heart. What do YOU want? I know hearing our own voice is challenging, but the only way you'll get good at it is by practicing. God gave us intuition, which I believe is how He speaks softly to us. We just have to be still long enough to listen.

I certainly didn't jump right into my decision. I took over thirty years. I did the hard work and was free long before the surgery. Give yourself permission to do something big for yourself. Maybe you need to leave a toxic situation or change jobs. Perhaps you want to learn to sky dive or scuba dive. Do you want to travel abroad? Or like me, maybe some plastic surgery is on your bucket list. Don't wait for other's approval. Life is so very short. My parents never traveled because they were saving it for their retirement. Well, that day never came; they both died young.

Live Your FIT Life

Like anything, we must balance our desire to do things our way with meeting the needs of others. I believe when we practice self-care, we are more capable of giving to others more fully. When we run on empty, we have nothing left for others. The things we wish to do certainly shouldn't harm others, and they shouldn't go against our values or morals. Too often, though, we aren't being authentic. We are living a lie. We are living someone else's life. If you are a mom, you should have a greater motivation to turn that around. What message do we send our young ladies if we sacrifice ourselves for the sake of someone else? I see this too often. Women become obese in the name of taking care of their kids. Hogwash! This sends the wrong message completely. We are telling our kids women are good for making babies and have no worth outside of that. Please, if you can't do this for yourself, do it for your children!

You've read through most of my book, and I hope the message is clear: You can start improving the quality of your life today. Don't delay another minute. Do SOMETHING. You will be glad you did, and so will others in your life. I promise. If by chance, those closest to you get upset about your changes for the better, then you have surrounded yourself with the wrong people. Walk away from all the drama and the vampires. Choose to surround yourself with people who love you, support you, and cheer you on.

I encourage you to stick with your journey because you *will* have layers. Under each issue lies another. Don't be discouraged by this but see the upside—you are healing and improving layer by layer. Day by day, you are becoming something better. Some layers will be more painful than others, but remain faithful. They shall pass.

> *The thing always happens that you really believe in;*
> *and the belief in a thing makes it happen.*
> ~ Frank Lloyd Wright ~
> *Architect*

Believe

I know of two gals who came from very similar situations. They both came from very dysfunctional, unhealthy families and were both raped when younger. How they both handled it was quite different. One ignored her pain, suppressing it deep within her. She acted out her anger by being promiscuous and wild. She got into stripping, married and divorced numerous times, and had an abortion. To this day, in her forties, she is still running from her past. She is miserable and has alienated her good friends because of her continued drama. She is no further along the journey, repeating mistakes over and over again; she is stuck.

On the contrary, another other gal chose to look her pain square in the eye. She went into counseling, sought God with a vengeance, and dealt with her pain. It was not easy, and it involved many layers. Through the years, she got depressed, anxious, and ill during some of the layers. But she persisted. Today, in her forties, she is happily married with wonderful children. Whatever your past looks like, do not let it determine your tomorrow. You are *not* what you did years ago. You *can* live a different life.

You are not what you did years ago.

Make Every Day Count

Life is indeed short. The man who became like my father when I was thirteen (also my mentor with his wife) was diagnosed with a terminal brain tumor. The news hit me like a ton of bricks, and I was faced with a wave of emotions. Both my real parents died of cancer as well, so at first, I was very angry. I couldn't believe this was happening to me again. After hearing the news, I gave myself permission to be selfish and whine for an entire day. *Poor me! Why is this happening to me?* Blah, blah, blah. Although these are all very real emotions, I knew they would not help the situation in the long term. But I knew I needed to feel them. Once I gained my composure, I turned my attention toward what I could do for my "second dad." Being long distance, I started to pray. I prayed specifically, diligently, and relentlessly. This became my priority. He had spent 50 years in ministry serving others; his life was too valuable to this world. I wasn't going to give up! But here he was with an awful outlook.

Just because you are reading a book on how to get your life back doesn't mean life will cooperate. Just because I wrote a book on managing your life doesn't mean I'm guaranteed smooth sailing. In fact, I'd say it is just the opposite. As I mentioned earlier, when folks commit to losing weight, events will unfold that pack their schedules so tight that they have difficulty squeezing in exercise. Or when someone decides to simplify her life, a family member will need to move in for assistance. Life doesn't give any of us a break. And none of us get out of here alive.

When we embark on major changes that will have a huge positive impact on others and ourselves, be prepared for resistance. Every time I write a book, I brace myself. I can expect challenges in the very areas I am writing on. Situations will arise that force me to "practice what I preach." I consider it more material. I am in process, and so are you. When life hits you, fight back! This is your life. Use your tools and the power God has given you.

When life hits you, fight back!

In the case with my second dad and his brain tumor, prayer and faith were our tools. Between all of his family, we recruited thousands and thousands of friends and church members across the globe to pray. We also believed without doubt that he would be cured. You cannot have faith and doubt. I had to deliberately erase my fears and thoughts of possible death. I wasn't in denial but in true obedience to God's promises and trusted Him with every ounce of my being for His deliverance. Although he was given only three months to live, he lived another year. God provided a miracle! The lessons we all learned:

1. God is **all**-powerful.

2. God is **still** the great healer.

3. God **is** in control.

4. God is bigger than **all** our problems.

5. Prayer works.

6. Life is short—live it like there is no tomorrow!

Regardless of the situation or outcome, we must continue to have faith, believe, and trust God. Life is so short; we need to live it to the fullest.

Seize the Day

Why it takes such "big frying pans" over our heads to get our attention, I'll never know. But when you can, seize every moment you are given. We are not promised or guaranteed tomorrow. We have these moments, right here and now. We can spend these moments whining or complaining, becoming a victim like so many women I see. They blame their parents, husbands, and society for their problems, because it is easier than looking in the mirror and admitting their part. Being a victim will only keep you in the dark and prevent you from experiencing God's light. Nothing in your life will change for the better; it will only get worse. Instead, choose to be joyful. I'm not suggesting that we operate like robots. We are humans with emotions, and we need to feel them. Just be sure you don't get stuck in any one negative emotion for too long.

A friend of mine was coming to visit one day, and she woke up in a "funk." She really didn't feel like getting ready to come exercise with me, but she decided to lock her "funk in her trunk" and drove over anyway. We had a really fun workout together, and her spirits were lifted. When she opened her trunk back up, her funk was gone—smothered to death. Don't let negative emotions prevent you from experiencing all God has for you, and He has a world full!

What poison is to food, self-pity is to life
~ OLIVER C. WILSON ~
American percussionist

Stay on the Path

The world isn't going to change, however, just because we are trying so very hard to improve. The reality is that the world will seem harsher, faster, and more out of control to you once you regain some sense of order. Stress will never go away; we can never get rid of it completely. What we can do, though, is respond to it in healthier ways. That is really the bottom line of this book—a formula to equip you with alternative ways of coping with life. We have all tried the other ways, and they simply don't work long term. Food won't comfort you; it will only make you gain weight. Alcohol won't make the pain go away; it will only numb your senses, making it easier for you to make additional mistakes. Smoking won't really take your mind off your troubles; it will only deprive you of oxygen so you can't think straight. Avoiding pain doesn't make it go away; it makes it ten times bigger and more stressful. The list goes on. Whatever unhealthy way you have used in the past to manage your stress is only adding to the problem.

You've started on a new path; stay on it. I love the Christmas cartoon *The Year without a Santa Claus*. It's the one that has Mother Nature's children, Mr. Heat Miser and Mr. Cold Miser, and everyone tries to help give Santa a day off. Anyway, during the song where Kris Kringle is helping the Snow Monster learn to walk, he sings a song: "Put one foot in front of the other, and soon you'll be walking out the door." It's a cute song with a serious reminder for us that little steps, one by one, get us there.

> *Victory is won not in miles, but in inches.*
> *Win a little now, hold your ground,*
> *and later win a little more.*
> ~ LOUIS L'AMOUR ~
> *Novelist*

So often society pushes and almost demands immediate results. With microwaves, drive-through windows, and instant messaging, the world is literally moving faster. When I was writing my first book, I emailed my friends my exciting news the day the contract was signed. Two weeks later, a friend of mine emailed me back and asked, "So are you done writing your book yet?" People are losing the ability to slow down and understand that some things, important things, do take time. When I was going through my divorce, I had a "friend" tell me after two weeks that she had enough. I was to call her when I was "over this" and would be more fun again. The world is crazy. Just because we are in the world doesn't mean we have to be *of* it. We can set our own pace, and I believe we are called to.

Lead the Way

If we don't show an example of a better way, who will? Our children need to know that another way exists. It isn't enough to say something is the wrong way; we must give an option. The best way to ensure that someone understands is to show them. As you develop your new life that is more balance, share your experiences with others. If you find something in this book extremely helpful, pass it on.

Education is learning what you didn't
even know you didn't know.
~ DANIEL BOORSTIN ~
Historian

Slow down as much of your life as you can. Do you remember being a teenager waiting for a big dance or event to come up and saying to your parents, "Oh, I'm so bored? Time is going too slow"? I think every parent has told a child, "Just wait until you are older. Time will fly by so fast your head will spin." Boy, they weren't kidding. The weeks go faster, and the months click away in a flash. The more you can bring control back, the more enjoyable your life will be. You won't feel like you are missing out or watching from the outside in—you will be in your life. You will have more of a say of what you do with your time, and that is creating the life YOU want. Then you will have even more time to learn and grow.

Keep Learning

I know I'm still learning as I'm on the journey, too. You will have your own experiences to share with others. Every day presents the opportunity for a new situation to arise. What worked for one challenge may not work for another, so we will constantly be applying and learning new ways to manage stress. Besides life throwing new things at us, people are ever changing. How we handle a person one time may not work the next because they, too, are on a journey. It's like the cartoon that says, "Just when I figured out all the answers, they changed the questions!" The way to look at it is this: When we stop learning, we die.

Here's an excerpt from a neat poem:

I've learned that
we are responsible for what we do,
no matter how we feel.
I've learned that
you can either control your attitude
or it controls you.
I've learned that
heroes are the people who
do what has to be done,
regardless of the consequences.
I've learned that
it isn't always enough to be forgiven by others.
Sometimes you have to learn to forgive yourself.
I've learned that
maturity has more to do with

> *what types of experiences you've had*
> *and what you've learned from them*
> *and less to do with how many birthdays*
> *you've celebrated.*
> *I've learned that*
> *our background and circumstances*
> *may have influenced who we are,*
> *but we are responsible for who we become.*
> ~ KATHY KANE HANSEN ~
> *Writer*

Trust God

Who we become is a combination of the choices we make and God's hand in our lives. When we are wondering where in the world is God and why He isn't fixing something, He is usually waiting for us to take action. When we do, He is right there besides us, helping us get through. He knows our circumstances and *who* we can become, because He has created us. He has faith in us. We must trust Him.

As you create new habits, patterns, thoughts, and beliefs, have faith that God will assist you. You know the "Footprints in the Sand" story, right? When we see only one set of footprints in the sand, it is because He is carrying us. When you get weary on your journey, which you will, lean on Him. When you are worried the trip isn't going as you planned, pray for peace. Know that God has been on your side all along, and so am I. We're both rooting for you and cheering you on as you defy your diagnosis and create your FIT life.

DEFY YOUR DIAGNOSIS CHAPTER THIRTEEN

FIT Life Formula @ Work

What do you want more of this year?

What do you want less of this year?

What's the biggest mistake you made last year?

What ONE thing would bring you huge amounts of joy? What are you waiting for?

CHAPTER FOURTEEN

Defy Your Diagnosis!

Whatever we expect with confidence
becomes our own self-fulfilling prophecy.
~ BRIAN TRACY ~
Public speaker

By now, you know I am no stranger to adversity. In my twenties, I was told I would live in pain and never run again due to bulging discs, which have been completely repaired through chiropractic care, acupuncture, and yoga (X-rays show a normal and healthy spine now). In my thirties, I went misdiagnosed for six years, suffering from incredible pain, swelling, and bizarre symptoms doctors couldn't figure out. My correct diagnosis of Lyme disease didn't make things better. In fact, many believe you cannot cure Lyme disease, and those who do will tell you curing Lyme disease makes you worse before you get better. Recently, Lyme disease is being compared to cancer: just as difficult to diagnose, and when they do, good luck beating it. If you do kill it off before it kills you, you are forever changed. For three years, I underwent treatment, followed by another three years of recovery—and this was quick compared to most (usually takes as long as you had the disease to get over it). I doubled up my treatments, combing antibiotics with natural alternatives. This made the poisoning effect twice as severe. My philosophy was if I was going to suffer, I might as well be totally miserable and get it over with!

Being a fitness professional and personal trainer, I understood the importance of nutrition and exercise. I continued to work, exercise, and committed to a healthy lifestyle to fight the wicked intruder who invaded my body. In 2010, I celebrated being Lyme and pain-free by running a marathon. I certainly didn't break any speed records, but I completed the 26.2 miles without pain. Victory! Life was good until …

Déjà Vu

In 2013, I swelled up. Within three months, I went from a hard-core fitness enthusiast to a person who couldn't pull up her own pants. I couldn't pull or push anything. I couldn't even start my own car or lock a door. Unlike Lyme disease, this wasn't jumping around from joint to joint but settled squarely into my finger joints, specifically my index and middle finger knuckles—classic rheumatoid arthritis symptoms. Tests confirmed I no longer had the *Borrelia burgdorferi* bacteria in my body, yet I was suffering once again. My energy plummeted, and I had zero strength.

My experience with traditional medical doctors has not been favorable. Many are a hammer that only sees a nail. Whatever their specialty, they often will diagnose you with it. That is how they make their money. However, my naturopath was out of ideas. We had tried every natural option, including, but not limited to: minerals, supplements, diet changes, rest, stress management, acupuncture, and massage. The time had come for blood tests by a rheumatologist.

I knew this was serious, and I dreaded the outcome. I went with apprehension. The tests were taken, and when I met with the rheumatologist, she confirmed my greatest fear: Lyme disease damaged my immune system, giving me RA. I went home and screamed in anguish. This time, I did sit in the corner and cried. I wasn't sure I could go through another battle for my life, yet here I was.

When I asked the doctor if she was sure I had RA, she replied, "A normal rheumatoid factor is below fourteen. Yours is beyond what we can even measure, well above three hundred fifty." Damn. As much as I wasn't a fan of traditional medical doctors, I couldn't deny the facts. The doctor sat me down and said my RA could eventually cause blindness, and most people die young from failed organs due to the drugs taken to treat the disease. "But," she said with a smile, "you will be able to live a normal life while on the RA drugs." She also told me one drug wasn't going to be strong enough in the long term due to my severe case. In short time, I would require additional medications, all of which had horrific side effects. My chances of cancer would increase 70 percent, and I would basically lose all ability to fight off ANYTHING, because the medications would shut down my immune system completely. They would do nothing about the problem but simply manage the symptoms. I was discouraged, to say the least. I took home all the literature, read it thoroughly, and proceeded to throw it out in the trash. I am a fighter, as you have read, and I was going to beat this, too!

I reset my immune system by using LDN (low-dose naltrexone). Most commonly used for drug addicts, LDN cleans your cells of receptors. In the case of drug addicts, it provides a short window of time where the body doesn't crave the drug. The idea is to give the addict a shot at working on why they are using drugs in the first place, without the desperate need for the substance. In autoimmune cases, it eliminates the receptors telling the body to attack itself. This, combined with anti-inflammatory treatment, a healthy diet, exercise, and rest gave my body a chance to heal and defy my diagnosis!

I had a couple of good years before I met menopause, and I've decided she is one MEAN girl and I don't like her very much. She gets mad without really knowing why, and the next moment she might be sad for no apparent reason. She doesn't like sleep much and rather toss and throw my body around like a sack of potatoes just for kicks and giggles. She is no laughing matter and demands respect. Ignore her at your own peril!

Who would have thought that we could have wrinkles AND acne at the same time? You'd think that getting gray hair on your head would mean less hair on your face. No such luck! Since men are wearing buns, is it acceptable for women to have goatees? I'm confident I could grow one in a day or two.

When I wrote my *Fit Over 50* book several years ago, I had not yet entered the "transition." I did a ton of research, though, to understand the process and get a clue as to what to expect. My goal at the time was simply to *reach* fifty, since so many in my family died young.

Well, here I am. I made it and have lived to go through one heck of a roller coaster of a ride—weak one moment, feeling strong the next, losing weight and gaining it right back. I've become my own floatation device, and it is a good thing since I can sweat enough to cause my own lake now. What I'm learning is that the information I found for my book is still valid, however, we have learned so much more. And like anything, we are all made different. That's what makes approaching this so difficult—one solution does not fit all. Add to this the fact that life is just much more stressful than years gone by. Cortisol wreaks havoc on your already fluctuating hormones causing additional weight gain. Oh joy!

Some women seem to sail through menopause without a hiccup. I'm trying not to hate them. Others have it way worse than me, and I send my condolences. What I want to do is kick menopause in her ever-growing butt, but with my luck, I'd pull a muscle in the process. Instead, I'm choosing to focus on the positive. I am alive and given the opportunity to age, albeit not so graceful at times. I am grateful for my naturopath as she partners with me to ease me through my transition. I guess it is kind of exciting. What will I be on the other side? Will menopause and I become friends? In the meantime, I take a day at a time.

We All Have Stuff

Perhaps you are fortunate enough not to have been diagnosed with an incurable disease. If so, consider yourself blessed. I believe we all have stuff that we accept that just isn't true, though, and our own attitudes and judgments limit us and negatively impact our lives, causing unnecessary suffering. I have learned a great deal through all my pains, and I want to share it with you. First, I have something to ask of you.

We all bring our own backgrounds, attitudes, and beliefs with us wherever we go. Some have served us well, and others have prevented us from reaching our full potential. If we are truly going to beat something, we need to make room for new ideas and possibilities. What I would like from you will only take a moment. Below, I want you to write down your Negative Nelly or Ned. You know, the voice inside your head that pooh-poohs new ways of doing things. It often creates negative thoughts and attitudes about things before you really have all the facts. Sometimes it is fear, doubt, untrustworthiness, skepticism, anger, or a judgmental attitude.

By signing this, you are agreeing to keep an open mind to receive and consider a new way of approaching the tough times of life.

Name: _____

My Negative Nelly (or Ned) is: _____

I hereby agree to quiet my Negative Nelly or Ned while I read this chapter so I may keep an open mind and explore new ways of approaching my tribulations.

I know I can listen to my Negative Nelly or Ned after I am done, if I so choose.

Signed: _____

Date: _____

Steps to Defy Your Diagnosis

Thank you! Now that you've put aside that negative voice, let's talk about the diagnosis. Hearing the news that you have an incurable disease from a medical professional you trust is devastating. Facing a divorce, loss of job, or death of a loved way takes the wind right out of your sails. To learn that I had beaten one incurable disease only to end up with another was overwhelming, and I had a flood of emotions assaulting me. I wanted to crawl in a hole and die. I told my husband I just didn't have it in me to fight another war. My choices were to give up and die in that hole, or get up and fight. Like the song by Lee Ann Womack says, "I hope you dance."

1. Define Your Diagnosis

The first principle, therefore, is that we must first determine and **define** our diagnosis. That sounds easy enough, but it isn't. Trust me. I had every medical professional telling me no cure exists for Lyme disease or RA. I was doomed by their standards. The key here is to NOT accept a cookie-cutter diagnosis and prognosis from anyone else but yourself. Although all my tests concluded I had a severe case of rheumatoid arthritis (my body was attacking and destroying my own joints) and I couldn't deny my pain, I could define my diagnosis to be one of a *curable* disease. I chose to believe in alternative options and believed in restoring my health. I had to quiet my own Negative Nelly!

A profound book called *You Are the Placebo* by Dr. Joe Dispenza shares the science behind the power of the mind. It's an intellectual read with a powerful story. In a nutshell, Dr. Dispenza's spine was crushed in a bicycle accident, and he was told he would never walk again. He defied his diagnosis differently than the doctors treating him and took an alternative route of care. He checked himself out of the hospital and treated himself, starting with him mind. Today, he rides, runs, and climbs! He defied his diagnosis by defining it differently.

The point here is that we have incredible power in our thoughts. What we think turns into our attitudes. These attitudes over time become our belief system. Our belief system guides and directs our actions. One of my favorite poems is called "Don't Quit." I keep the entire poem in my day planner, but I wanted to share a line that I chanted over and over again to remind myself to keep fighting the battle:

> *Stick to the fight when you are hardest hit.*
> *It's when things seem the worst*
> *That you must not quit!*
> ~ ANONYMOUS ~

We cannot deal with or overcome anything if we do not even know what it is. For medical ailments, do your homework and become an expert on your illness. I know way more about Lyme disease, RA, and menopause than I ever cared to know. Don't take just the word of one professional; seek several opinions. Regardless of your situation (physical, mental, professional, or relational), you must get honest with yourself and know what negative attitudes you are holding on to. What fears are lurking in the recesses of your mind? What false beliefs have you accepted? What barrier is preventing you from moving forward?

In my case, believing doctors knew everything was limiting my ability to see alternative solutions. Certainly, specialists and medical experts know a lot, but we are far more complex than any one human can comprehend. I was raised to never, ever question doctors. Then I learned to question everything, because it's my body and life! I decided to believe another way existed that didn't involve taking drugs that would only treat my symptoms.

Case in point: Having gone misdiagnosed for six years with Lyme disease, I am no stranger to the frustration of our medical system. I was told my illness was in my head for years. Meanwhile, I kept getting worse with crippling pain and deformity. Eventually, I found a healthcare provider willing to listen, test, and work toward getting me functioning again. So when I started having health issues two years ago, warning bells went off. Something was wrong, and I knew it. Unfortunately, I had also started going through menopause at the same time. Instead of being told it was all in my head this go around, they just said, "You're getting old and going through menopause. It's miserable. Get used to it."

Once again, I have been utterly disappointed and appalled at the lack of care and the shear laziness of the medical community. No one listened. I rattled off all my symptoms and my concerns, and I got blank looks of so-called professionals who just wanted to move on to their next patient. I could see it in their face: *Quit whining! Just accept that you will be fat, have no energy, and go bald.* Even worse, I asked tons of women for advice, and they all shrugged their shoulders. "This is just how it goes." How utterly sad that we accept poor health as normal or okay!

I chased down all sorts of things like mold illness, food allergies, and cortisol poisoning, just to name a few. All my blood work was normal. I was healthy … NOT! After two years of my own research, I stormed the gates and demanded help. I eventually found an endocrinologist who was willing to separate out menopause (which, by the way, I went through quickly) from the equation, listen to my complaints, and look at what was going on in MY body. Remember, all norms for blood work are just that. It means some of us might be lower or higher, but the average falls in the middle.

This was the case with my thyroid tests. They kept coming back "normal," even though I had all the symptoms of hypothyroid. The classic systems (all of which I exhibited but one):

- Extreme fatigue (I couldn't and still struggle getting up in the morning and have zero endurance.)

- Very dry, flaky skin (I had been feeling like a reptile.)

- Massive loss of hair (More than half exited my head in a month and is falling out in handfuls.)

- Unexplained weight gain that comes on rapidly (I put on 15 pounds in 1½ weeks while I was reducing my caloric intake AND exercising excessively. No matter what I've done, the weight continues to pile on.)

- Swelling of the face (My nose is twice its normal size.)

- Ringing in your ears or tinnitus (There are lots of causes of ear ringing, so I am unsure if my thyroid issues caused it or not. I'll probably never really know, but I wish I could answer the ring and make it stop!)

- Difficulty sleeping (What is sleeping through the night?)

- Cold hands and feet (I live in Phoenix, yet my hands and feet feel like ice cubes.)

- Joint and muscle pain (I hurt ALL the time.)

- Depression (Well, of course I'm upset—no one would listen!)

- Brain fog (thankfully, I've been functioning okay.)

If I had a dollar for every time I mentioned these symptoms, I wouldn't have to worry about my medical bills! Not one person considered the possibility that I had thyroid issues (even when I told them that thyroid problems run in my family) simply because the "bell rang" (that is, my tests were normal). Well, when you look at my history, my thyroid has been getting worse, but my levels still fall in the normal category. Everyone missed it except for me.

The point I am making here is twofold:

1. *Trust your gut!* You know when something is wrong. Don't settle for pat answers or a lazy diagnosis. Keep pursuing it until you feel better and get the proper diagnosis, care, and treatment.

2. *Don't accept being miserable, because menopause probably isn't the cause.* Yes, it can create problems; however, I'm learning that

upwards of 60 percent of women actually have thyroid issues but don't get the help they need due to being told, "It's menopause. Deal with it." Tragic!

If you are doing the right things yet not seeing results with your fatigue, weight gain, or hair loss, seek out an endocrinologist who is willing to have a discussion. They are difficult to find but exist. Our system, unfortunately fosters quick fixes and cheap resolutions. Providers aren't bad people but caught in a rat race they will never win. Stand your ground and voice your concerns. Feeling tired all the time isn't normal, and we aren't doomed to be obese when as we age when we live an active lifestyle. I encourage you to be brave enough to seek solutions. Know this: It isn't in your head, and you aren't alone! I wish you good luck and hope you, too, can be healthier and happier!

2. Identify Your Intentions

Once we define our diagnosis as we see fit, the next principle is to **identify** our intentions. I'm going to be blunt, because let's face it—some people do not want to get well. I know those are harsh words to hear, but I have met too many people who get significance from their problems. They identify with it and label themselves as stuck. They rather talk about their illness than seek help. For whatever reason, they rather complain about being overweight instead of exercising. Some want to take drugs rather than change their eating habits. Some stay in toxic relationships. In essence, their Negative Nelly or Ned is living rent-free in their head and is bossing them around.

I'm not judging anyone here. For crying out loud, I stayed with a man I didn't love who abused me mentally, emotionally, physically, and spiritually for six years. We must get honest and serious if we are going to be victors. Only you can decide when it is time to kick out those freeloaders and take your life back! I choose to take all the power I had back and use it for my good. My intentions were very clear: great health with absolutely no sign of any disease and zero pain. I did not want to take their drugs, only to ultimately get worse and die young. I intended to fight my battle creatively.

I love the TV series *Blue Bloods*. The show is about members of the Reagan family—some police officers and others attorneys—who have dedicated their lives to protecting and serving others. It is a mix of crime drama and family dynamics along with all-American values and faith. The Reagans are not perfect but put family first, pray to God, and try to do right by all. Tom Selleck, the main character, is the head of the family and New York City Police Commissioner. In one episode, his granddaughter Nicky goofs up and lets a friend hang out to dry at school because she was overwhelmed by peer pressure. She then feels horrible about her letting a friend down and hurting her feelings. Her uncle Jamie listens and then responds, "It is what you do next that matters." She stands by her friend despite the fact that she actually created the problem in the first place and extends grace and love.

Life is full of obstacles, many of which we will have no control over. What we do after a diagnosis or life pain is what matters. Do we deny it or blame others? Do we brush it off with sarcasm and justification? Or do we look it head on, facing it with courage and determination? We will each outline different courses for our unique circumstances, but we must be very intentional and deliberate with our actions. That brings us to the next principle: accelerate your actions.

3. Accelerate Your Actions

Researching is required, and taking a few steps is a start. However, if you truly want to defy your diagnosis, you have to be willing to go to extreme measures. When your Negative Nelly (or Ned) tries to take you down, you must shut her (or him) up. Forces of the universe will attack you, trying to pull you back into the pit of despair. You have to be prepared to ward them off, remain strong, and get serious.

True success is overcoming the fear of being unsuccessful.
~ PAUL SWEENEY ~
Attorney & author

Whatever your issue is, you might have to think outside of the box, as I did, and create a protocol or solution that doesn't exist yet. You will need to face your fears on a regular basis. Just because we define our diagnosis and identify our intentions does not mean we won't be scared. We are human beings, after all. I had days where I was consumed by the thought of never being able to walk again, no less run or hike. I knew I was taking the right actions, but doubts would creep in. What I was doing to cure my RA had never been done. I partnered with health practitioners who supported me. And I developed my own protocol based upon a lot of research while praying God would bless my efforts.

I envisioned my disease to be a foreign invader in my body. Well, actually, it was! To be exact, I pictured it as a gruesome monster. I kept exercising despite my pain and would yell at it, "Get out! You don't belong here!" When I taught my kickboxing class, I would envision every punch giving a crushing blow to the enemy within. I'll spare you some of the choice words I used. Suffice it to say, I harnessed my anger and placed is directly at my illness.

Going against the current in any situation can be freaking terrifying! When I shared my protocol with some folks, they looked at me like I had horns coming out of my head and came from another planet. The rheumatologist got angry with me and said, "You will end up in a wheelchair, and you deserve it!" History is full of examples of ordinary people overcoming extraordinary circumstances. We are the commanders of our own life. Once you commit to taking aggressive action, seek like-minded individuals to partner with along the path. You may need to eliminate some "vampires" in your life—you know, those people who suck you dry with their negativity! Feed your mind, body, and spirit with only positive nourishment.

As for me, I never went back to the rheumatologist (you think?) and chose to work with a naturopath instead. I'm here to tell you that all things are possible with the right thoughts, attitudes, beliefs, and actions. My blood work today shows not a single sign of RA, and I have been symptom and pain-free for almost seven years and counting without any drugs. I am back to playing tennis, pulling, pushing, exercising, and living an active life—free from pain. I do not have RA. I defied my diagnosis, and so can you!

4. Have Faith for Your Future

I would be remiss if I didn't tell you that my faith was a huge part of my healing process. I know God walked my journey with me, often carrying me when I didn't have the strength to go on or the load was just too heavy. My trust in Him allowed me to believe a healthier life was possible. A book that might interest you is *A More Excellent Way* by Henry W. Wright. I don't agree with everything in the book, but it is full of thought-provoking concepts. The author spent countless years researching the Bible and has spent his entire life healing people through prayer and Scripture. What he found is every disease is tied to some negative behavior, thought, or belief. He suggests RA, for instance, is caused by self-hatred and low self-esteem. The body begins to attack itself because a person hates themselves and doesn't feel worthy. Uh, that's me! Granted, I know that Lyme disease caused my immune system to malfunction, but that it honed in on attacking my own joints makes sense in light of this speculation. Again, you may or may not find it interesting or helpful.

A few years ago, I had both feet operated on. Lyme disease has residual effects, and I had huge tumors grow in the bottom of my feet called Morton's neuromas. I suffered with pain for five years and did every alternative I could before surgery was my last option. When my podiatrist sat me down and prepared me for the process, he said something that has forever stuck with me. For a surgery to be successful, three parties must do their part. First, he committed to giving his best skill and ability to me. Second, I needed to promise to be a good patient and do what would help my body heal and recover. Third is what he called the "God factor." Doctors are not gods. They can only do their best. We certainly live with our bodies, but God made them, and everyone is different. Well, he did an excellent job, I listened and followed my post-op instructions, and God showed up. I am now pain-free and living my active lifestyle.

I have since decided to call this the Healing Trinity. Whatever we face from the common cold to major illnesses, the Healing Trinity is involved. We cannot expect the medical community to operate outside of their scope of practice, nor can we demand miracles from them. They are only human. We most certainly must do our part. If we aren't happy with our health, then we need to look no further than the mirror and stop blaming others. What we do or don't do contributes more than anything to our overall health. You do know that 70 percent of the aging process is in our control, right? That means only 35 percent is out of our hands.

We cannot leave out the God factor. He made us and can heal us. He is the Great Physician and Miracle Maker. My faith gave me hope, and I pray He is your strength as well.

The Healing Trinity
- The right medical partner
- Doing your best
- Trusting God

5. Seek Support

I shared earlier how important it is to surround yourself with the right people. It is so critical that I am mentioning it again. I believe God often works through others. When we are in the midst of tough times, we can tend to pull away and isolate ourselves. I was certainly guilty. I didn't tell friends and family about my illness until I was about over it. Even clients didn't know. I thought I was being tough, but in reality, I suffered silently. I didn't allow others to love and support me. How could they pray for me when they didn't even know?

My journey to a full recovery was a lonely one, and I don't

recommend it. I was taught to keep personal traumas private. I learned from my mother, who learned from her mother. I failed to understand how giving blesses both parties. When we don't allow others to give, we prevent them from receiving a blessing. I am a very independent person, so one of the hardest lessons was allowing others to help me. To this day, I still struggle with asking for help, but I know God wants us to help with each other's burdens.

A caution here: Be selective with who you select to support you. Be sure you have realistic expectations of them. Some people are incapable of caring for anyone but themselves. Just because you need them doesn't mean they will respond favorably. I learned that the hard way, too. Better to have a close circle of friends than a large group of acquaintances!

Support groups can be encouraging, but ensure they are focused on full recovery rather than just living with your miserable disease. Too often, they are sponsored by drug companies who want you to take their drugs for the rest of your life because they make billions of dollars. They don't want you to get better. Did you hear me? Close to 50 percent of ALL people with autoimmune diseases actually have undiagnosed Lyme disease. This doesn't make the news, nor does it get funding to treat. Why? All those autoimmune drugs make billions and billions each year. No one gets better, but the pharmaceutical companies get rich. The treatment to cure Lyme, and frankly RA, isn't expensive, so it won't be publicized. That's a whole different book! If you want to have a conversation someday about how I overcame them both, contact me.

Always listen to experts. They'll tell you
what can't be done, and why. Then do it.
~ Robert A. Heinlein ~
Author of Time Enough for Love

Defy Your Diagnosis!

Back to my marathon: Like I said, I was not breaking any speed records. I was putting one foot in front of the other! God was with me, though, as the sun came up over the Rocky Mountains. I had hymns playing on my MP3 player and watched as the wildlife began waking up. (We started at 3:30 a.m.!) About halfway through my marathon, I needed to adjust my shoes and loosen up my shoe laces, as my feet had swollen from the constant impact. I pulled over to the shoulder of the road and began fixing my shoes. For your information, that is why runners buy their shoes a size or so bigger. It is natural on long runs to have your feel swell. Unbeknownst to me, I had a group of runners behind me. I could have sworn I was the caboose. I really was running slow and thought everyone else was already enjoying a nice warm meal. As they approached, they pleaded with me, "Please don't stop or give up! You've been our motivator for keeping going! We've been following you, and you've helped us keep pace."

Apparently, I wasn't dead last! I was just focused on putting one foot in front of the other. I was running my race, after all, with my goals and objectives to finish and feel great. I did not want to be one of those people who pissed blood or lost all their toe nails. True stories! I smiled and told the group of runners I was just adjusting my shoes, and they collectively breathed a sigh of relief and thanked me. As I began running again, I knew I wasn't just running my race now. I was leading a pack of runners to their finish line. My race was no longer just about me but a common goal. And although I did not ask for the position, I was leading people to their victory. We ultimately crossed the finish line together.

This is why I share my story and why I dedicate my life to improving the quality of people's lives. I want you to know you aren't alone and that someone else has gone before you and came out the other side. Hope DOES exist! Whether you have been diagnosed with an autoimmune disorder, disease, or difficult life event, I encourage you to explore alternative ways of approaching your challenge. Look for creative solutions that get you REAL results. Do the research and decide for yourself. If you don't like a particular doctor, coach, or counselor get another. Consider signing up for my FREE newsletter at my website (www.lorrainebosse-smith.com/resources/newsletter/) and take a look at all the resources available on my site designed to inspire, support, and encourage you as you defy *your* diagnosis! Here's to a healthier, happier you as you get your life back.

DEFY YOUR DIAGNOSIS CHAPTER FOURTEEN

FIT Life Formula @ Work

What is going on in your life right now that you need to define differently?

Are you willing to go to extreme measures to defy it? Write out the steps you will take:

Who is your inner circle support team? List them out and thank God for them!

Using the Healing Trinity model, write out your prayer here to the Great Physician:

Keep Standing!

After the storm comes tranquility.
~ UNKNOWN ~

I love to hear or read stories of others who have faced immense obstacles and challenges who conquer and overcome them to great victories. Our American history is full of such examples, and so is my life. I, along with you, have faced adversities of all kinds. You may not have related with my stories exactly, but I believe you received the message loud and clear: you can and will get through your storm.

Life Is Full of Storms

My life has not been a quiet or boring one. No sir. Through the years, I have shared some of my storms in books and magazines. Many people have read about them and commented, "My, you've been through a lot." My response? "More than some, but less than others." I know full well that, although I have had challenges, plenty of people face adversity every day. We cannot compare our unique situation to what someone else is facing. Even if we were both going through a similar crisis, we are each made differently with special coping mechanisms. Countless times, I have seen someone else suffering through something that would probably kill me, yet they courageously overcome their circumstance. Other people have said they just couldn't function or manage with what I've been through; we are all made different. I believe if the entire world could place all their troubles in one pile and we each were able to select our problem, we would probably grab the one we put in. Once we really saw the burdens others were carrying, we would gladly take our own situation back. Why? Because we know how to deal and cope with our own stuff. Thus the saying, "God doesn't give us more than we can handle." This doesn't mean awful stuff doesn't happen to us; rather, we are equipped and able to face our adversity.

Tough Out Turbulent Times

Yes, I have been through some wicked storms. I truly thought some would kill me; others really did try to take me out of the game. With God's help, I persevered. I learned a lot, and my hope is by sharing my stories and my Fit Life Formula that you can embrace your own and commit to fight hard and win!

Battles take their toll on us. Knowing what we need is paramount to our healing. Unfortunately, we can often lose ourselves in bad situations. Women in particular spend so much of their lives pleasing other people they have many voices rattling around in their heads. Ever try to quiet them down? Not easy! I encourage you to start listening for your own small voice, usually way off in the distance. Pay heed to it, and with practice, you will begin to know yourself again.

If you get lost, you can always be found.
~ PHILLIPS PHILLIP ~
Singer & songwriter

When we face tough times, we often go into "survival" mode. Thankfully, this coping mechanism helps us push through. The cost can be great, however, and we must be sure to recover once the storm passes.

Rediscover Yourself

Even though we live with ourselves, the reality is we can and do get lost, forgetting what we are really like. We bend and adapt beyond recognition. Many give up things they love for the wrong people. This is the opportunity for you to reclaim those aspects of your life. A tool I recommend for learning how you are wired is DISC, a human-behavior model. See the resources section for many great books, but if you are interested in figuring out your particular style, get a copy of *Leveraging Your Communication Style* by myself and Dr. John Jackson. The assessment will only take twenty minutes, but you will gain insights into your dominant style, how you communicate, your typical approach to things, and how to recover from stress, which is important during your healing. You will be reminded of who you are supposed to be and your strengths. Focus on using those strengths to get you through and recover from your storm.

Standing Stones

God made us and knows us intimately. And thankfully, He loves us anyway! He knew we would need encouragement through the valleys of life, and that is why thousands of years ago, people began erecting standing stones: a monument of tall stones serving as a reminder for all to see how something amazing happened here. After receiving the Ten Commandments, Moses erected standing stones after their miraculous crossing of the Jordan River (Joshua 4:2–3, 8–9). For thousands of more years to come, people will be reminded how God showed up and did something supernatural.

During the most difficult times of my life, God has not only showed up but often carried me when I did not have the strength to walk. Despite all I have been through, I am still standing! When I reflect and look back upon the many fierce storms that have crashed down upon me, I am quite amazed I am alive to tell about it. However, we have all faced storms; I know I am not unique. Your storms may be more violent than mine, or your storms may have lasted longer. One thing is for sure: Storms are a part of our lives—yours and mine. What separates us is what we do with and through those storms. What allows us to get back up when we have fallen is knowing we are not alone.

When you overcome an obstacle, you become a standing stone for someone else. You are their reminder of how God is still in the business of supporting, encouraging, and strengthening us. When you see someone else get up after a horrific battle, you know you can, too. Each new challenge also gives us compassion for one another. We truly understand the hurt and know that we know God can, and does, heal.

Forever Fit

One of my favorite fitness classes to teach is what I call Forever Fit. It is a low-impact, traditional aerobics class geared toward active, older adults or seniors. I had a great following when we lived in California, and some of my fondest memories are of teaching those classes. I'm grateful to be teaching that format again here in Phoenix. I am so inspired by folks in their sixties, seventies, and eighties who are still standing. In fact, they are moving, dancing, and living life to the fullest. Younger people pop into class from time to time, and they are put to shame by the elders in the group. Oh, how I smile! These folks are reminders to me of what a good attitude will get you.

This is why we can't keep our successes, victories, and triumphs to ourselves. We must share so that others can be encouraged. I love the biblical principle of Barnabus, Paul, and Timothy. Barnabus was an old man who invested in the younger generation. We all need seasoned viewpoints and wisdom. Paul was a peer who came alongside his friends, offering encouragement. And Timothy was a youngster just coming up through the ranks. Full of energy and hope, he had a new set of eyes but lacked experience. Our life should have all three, and we need to make an effort to be involved in other's lives. The lessons we learn shouldn't be kept a secret.

As iron sharpens iron, so one person sharpens another.

~ PROVERBS 27:17 ~

Here's a poem I wrote that I want to share with you:

I'M STILL STANDING

The rain came down in a violent force.
My boat was rocked completely off course.

But I was able to stand ...

The winds blew hard and powerfully.
I was knocked down and brought to my knees.

But I continued to stand ...

Just then the hail pounded me with no avail.
I began to get weak and slightly frail.

But I kept on standing ...

The ground trembled and shook me about.
I was utterly exhausted and filled with doubt.

But I chose to stand ...

I knew with You, my faith must stay,
even when the floods came to take me away.

Your strength, not mine, got me through.
I couldn't have made it without You!

Your love and grace are sufficient for me,
for I was blind but now I see!

So only because of You can I be considered a standing stone.
You never left me, and I was never alone.

I am *Still* Standing!

©Lorraine Bossé-Smith

The next time life knocks you down, remember all you have learned, who you are, and whose you are: You WILL stand again! Please know you aren't alone, and I genuinely wish you much happiness and good health. May you seek, find, and live a FIT Life!

CONCLUSION

FIT Life Formula @ Work

Recall a time when God delivered you from a situation:

List out other victories and answered prayers you have experienced:

Who is struggling right now and could use your encouragement? Commit to reaching out to them and sharing your Standing Stone story.

AFTERWORD

Full Disclosure

You're going to go through some tough times—
that's life. But I say, "Nothing happens to you;
it happens for you." See the positive in negative events.
~ JOEL OSTEEN ~
Pastor & bestselling author

As I have mentioned, I encountered extreme resistance in writing this book. I could not have foreseen all the obstacles that would be thrown in my path. In all honesty, if I had known, I would have probably surrendered, given up, and thrown my book project away. When friends start calling you Job, you know you are being attacked! Good gravy.

Two years of unemployment for my husband pushed us to the edge and brink of destruction. Couple that with my income tanking and bobbing around the bottom because of all my health issues, and we had a recipe for disaster. I don't know of anyone who could have sustained financially as long as we have. In fact, friends who recently lost one of their two incomes were freaked out after one month. Yeah, talk to me in two years! To the few who actually got the magnitude of our crisis, God bless you!

Originally, this book was pitched by my agent. Within eight months, he had a publisher. Right before the contract signature, the company was purchased, and my title was eliminated from their lineup. It was a blow, but I knew in my heart that non-traditional publishing was probably a better route for this book. For very conservative, Christian publishers, it may be a little edgy. Yet it is faith based, so other publishers may steer clear of it. The reality was, I had to make this happen on my own: me and God. Why should I be surprised? He and I have been walking together for a long time. Each and every time I am disappointed in a human or my circumstances, He reminds me He has my back. He IS my rock. I took a big step of faith by seeking crowdfunding, and my faith in humanity was restored. I was overwhelmed at the response and grateful to each person who contributed. Thank YOU!

Doubt crept in, though, and I began to second-guess myself. I mean, who was I kidding? My life is not perfect, and I don't always abide by my own advice. How can I encourage others when I am discouraged myself? As I worked on this book, I felt further away from my own message of hope. The weight of our stressful situation caused huge rifts between me and my husband, and I had more days than I care to admit when I just didn't want to get out of bed.

I've prided myself on being fit and trim my entire life. In years past when I was in difficult situations, I would stop eating. I know the great harm that approach causes, and I began stress-eating for the first time in my life, adding to the weight gained due to menopause and thyroid issues. I went from a size 6 to a size 10. This just added to my frustration and sadness, not to mention creating new pains in my knees and feet.

Dark days are no stranger to me, but this stage of life felt different. I felt I had no purpose, and we know that without purpose, people *will* perish. I was spiraling downward—fast. As I screamed for help and heard silence, my loneliness consumed me. I was not happy with who I was, where I was, what I looked like, and how I was handling it all.

The Stirring in My Heart

Just when I was ready to toss in the towel and burn my manuscript (even after the crowdfunding came in), God spoke to me. My spirit received this: *The very reason I chose you for this message is because you are imperfect. You were never expected to be without fault—just vulnerable, open, honest, and encouraging.* I also felt God reminding me that because of all my hurts, pains, struggles, mistakes, and doubts, I truly understand what others are going through.

This past Sunday, the message was about how God uses the broken, the ones with scars.

I have some incredibly large scars from my battle with Lyme disease. You may not see them, but they are very real. For far too long, I've been reminded of all that the disease robbed from me: my youth, health, children, business ventures, energy, and peace. If I continue to see the loss, then the disease continues to destroy my life. I've been working very hard on celebrating my scars. I am alive! I am walking when I was told I would be in a wheelchair, and I am living an active lifestyle despite the deformities it created. Every warrior has scars, so I choose to be proud of mine and the victories they represent. God can turn those wounds into scars and move us to better days. This is His message; I am just the vessel.

Leaning in Further

As I take a deep breath, lean in, and allow God's spirit to fill me up, His light penetrates all the dark corners that are the result of our trying times. I let go of my fears and anxieties. Nowhere in my book did I say I was perfect and led the ideal life. On the contrary, I hope you heard loud and clear that my life has been riddled with hardship. I can only write about the FIT Life Formula because I had to learn how to cope and conquer for myself. Each and every day, I utilize this formula, and God works through it to help and heal me.

My facing yet another challenging time gives me the opportunity to once again *Defy My Diagnosis*. I have encouraged you to get up when you are knocked down, and I will do the same. On good days, I manage my stress and display great courage. I continually listen for God's whisper and look for lessons all around me. I've managed to keep my sense of humor, and I am *still* standing.

I wanted to give you full disclosure so you didn't think that I have arrived. My FIT Life Formula works, but life is always changing. Just when I overcome one obstacle, another presents itself. Many of the usual tools will work, but I may need to seek new ones. I may suffer, but I believe who I become through the fire will always be a better version of myself. I look forward to seeing my new self on the other side of this one!

Be brave, dear ones. Create your FIT life, let go and let Go, and never, EVER give up.

With much love,

Lorraine Bossé-Smith
www.lorrainebosse-smith.com

Acknowledgements

Like anything worthwhile, this book required work. I have spent more time on this project than any of my other eight books … combined. I wasn't lacking material. On the contrary, just when I thought I was done with the manuscript, I would find myself in another life challenge that provided yet another chapter. It went from ten chapters to fourteen over the course of a couple of years. I finally had to say, "It is done" even when I wasn't quite sure it was finished.

The assaults and attacks were stronger than I've ever experienced, so I assume the message is important and needed. I certainly had opportunities to live out my own principles throughout the process—some days better than others. Without the prayer of friends, I would still be consumed by the chaos. Gordon Peterson, in particular, saw the vision for this book, and he encouraged me to go a step further from a small booklet to a book. Thank you for being a prayer warrior and a faithful friend.

To Susan Kerby, I am grateful for your belief in me and my message. You may not realize it, but you gave me courage just when I needed it—some wind beneath my wings—simply by being you.

I have too many long-distance friends to list them all, but to Lisa Buzas, Caroline McIntyre, Mary Horlock, Rachel Hulse, Cheryl Peterson, Jesscy Zimmerman, Karen Eade, and Tammy Young—I am blessed because of you! Through the ups and downs and sideways, I am glad to have you in my life. Thank you for loving me as I am.

To my Forever FIT class (present and past), you inspire me beyond words. Each time I come to give you a workout that improves your health, it is me who is receiving. Your smiles are gifts, and your positive attitudes contagious.

I appreciate everything Larry Carpenter and his team at Christian Book Services and Clovercroft Publishing have done to make this book a reality.

My family and I have certainly had our struggles—one of the greatest being the huge age gap between us—but they have remained my family, no matter what. Sometimes life thrust us into difficult situations, and other times we created our own strife. Chris, Jim, Nancy, Janice, and Jack, thank you for it all. Because of you, I've grown, matured, and learned the importance of family love—the good, the bad, and the Jimmy (ha).

The Smith family accepted me into their tribe on the day I married Steve back in 1998, and I am grateful.

To everyone who has donated and supported my crowdfunding campaign, you have my utmost gratitude. I couldn't have done this without your help! May we each defy our diagnosis every day and overcome any obstacle.

Book Lorraine Today!

Lorraine has competitive rates, provides a special discount to churches and nonprofits, and offers package deals to maximize your investment. Call for specifics today!

- *Transform Your Leadership Style*
- *Rewire Your Communication Style for Success*
- *Present to Any Audience*
- *Close the Sale at Hello*
- *Tackle Time Traps & Get More Done in Less Time*
- *Tame the Technology Monster*
- *Discover the Truth About Nutrition and Exercise*
- *Defy Your Diagnosis!*
- *Get Your Life Back!*
- *When Life Knocks You Down, Fight Back!*
- *Finally Get FIT!*
- *Balance Work & Life*
- *Stay Fit Over 50*

Lorraine Bossé-Smith
www.lorrainebosse-smith.com
(623) 582-1578

Make It A Healthy Year!

For CEOs to stay-at-home moms, this encouraging book provides 101 ways to lessen stress. Read it front to back or just pick a tip for today. A healthier life awaits you!

$10.00 each

Discouraged and frustrated because you can't find the right program or stick with it? Readers will take an exclusive assessment to determine their FIT (Fitness Individuality Trait) and then customize a new program to FINALLY reach their health goals. new you awaits! Perfect for anyone at any age!

$20.00 each

This book is for anyone who wants their next chapter of life to be their BEST one!

Uncover the myths and learn the truth about the aging process. You will be encouraged and inspired to develop a fitness program for your specific stage of life. It is NEVER too late to get healthy! Start today.

$20.00 each

Make It A Successful Year!

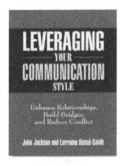

Learn how to be a master of communication by seeking to understand the four different communication styles. This book helps improve relationships at work or home. Get ready to reduce conflict and open the doorway to better communication and enhanced relationships. Build bridges, not walls.

$18.00 each

Regardless of your role, title, or position, people are looking to you for leadership. Discover your unique leadership style and learn how to identify other's styles to motivate, communicate, and lead people to greater achievements. Workbook now included!

$20.00 each

You have the education and experience required for the job. Now learn how to speak the language that will get you the job on the spot! This PDF file is fast yet informative.

$5.00 each

DVDs

Now you can have a safe, effective, and fun workout in the privacy of your own home with minimal equipment.

Lorraine Bossé-Smith is your personal trainer and coach as she guides you to tone up, trim down, stretch, and stabilize … all with encouragement that you can do it!

Each video is $20.00 and available on Lorraine's website: www.lorrainebosse-smith.com

Running times vary. Must select Data DVD on players or run on computer.

CPSIA information can be obtained
at www.ICGtesting.com
Printed in the USA
JSHW020535180420
5141JS00002B/4